Awakening To Messiah

MESSIANIC RABBI SCHNEIDER, HOST OF
"DISCOVERING THE JEWISH JESUS", SHARES HIS FAITH.

MESSIANIC RABBI K. A. SCHNEIDER

WESTBOW
PRESS
A DIVISION OF THOMAS NELSON

WestBow Press books may be ordered through booksellers or by contacting:

WestBow Press
A Division of Thomas Nelson
1663 Liberty Drive
Bloomington, IN 47403
www.westbowpress.com
1-(866) 928-1240

ISBN: 978-1-4497-0587-9 (sc)
ISBN: 978-1-4497-0609-8 (e)

Library of Congress Control Number: 2010937274

Printed in the United States of America

WestBow Press rev. date: 10/14/2010

Acknowledgements

I want to begin where I should by expressing my love and thankfulness to God my Father, Yeshua my Messiah, and the Ruach HaKodesh (Holy Spirit) whom this book is ultimately about. "Awakening To Messiah" is the result of the LORD's love and electing grace operating in my life.

Secondly, I want to acknowledge my wife Cynthia whom has been used by God to bring truth and healing into my life. Without her influence, I would not be who I am by God's grace today.

Thirdly, I want to thank my senior editor Cathy Hartman. Cathy worked hundreds of hours on this book. Her contribution in helping me articulate my thoughts, in grammar, and in her tireless spirit of encouragement cannot be overemphasized. Without Cathy, you would probably not be reading this book right now. In addition to all this, the LORD gave Cathy the title for this work, "Awakening To Messiah."

Lastly, I would like to express my appreciation to Katherine Palmer whom the LORD supernaturally connected me to. Kathy sacrificed her love, time and talent to elevate this book to a level of excellence that made it suitable to publish. Kathy is a professional transcriptionist.

Awakening To Messiah

Messianic Rabbi Kirt Schneider

When the word LORD is used, it is referring to the Hebrew name of God, Yahweh.

All New Testament scripture verses using the word *Christ* have been changed to the word *Messiah* and placed in parenthesis or brackets.

Contents

Chapter One

My Testimony

It is my desire to share with you my personal testimony as to how I, a Jewish person, came to the knowledge that Jesus (Yeshua) is the Messiah. In doing so, I pray it will give you a perspective you may not have considered regarding the salvation of Israel. I want to help you understand your role in bringing the message of Yeshua and God's Kingdom to the Jewish people. This is extremely important, because the LORD tells us in Romans 11 that when Jewish people do come to faith in Yeshua and call upon Him to return, it will be like "life from the dead" for all His people. What an awesome promise! Yeshua said this same thing in Matthew 23:39, speaking of Himself to the Jewish people, "You will not see Me again until you say, 'Blessed is He who comes in the name of the LORD.'" (In Hebrew: Baruch haba b'shem Adonai.)

I pray my testimony will also increase your faith in Yeshua. Oftentimes, I meet people who have gone to church their entire lives, who sincerely believe Yeshua is the Messiah; but deep in their minds, they question their faith. This sometimes happens when they observe people throughout the world who believe differently but are just as sincere in their beliefs. No matter what others in the world believe, the truth is Yeshua is indeed the Messiah. He is the Way, the Truth, and the Life, and no one comes to God but through Him.

CHILDHOOD YEARS

As a child, I was raised in Beachwood, a suburb of Cleveland, Ohio, in the heart of the Jewish community. Cleveland is one of the strongest Jewish populations in the country, although it isn't as big as New York City or Los Angeles. When I was growing up, Beachwood was approximately 90-95% Jewish; consequently, all my friends were Jewish. It wasn't that I sought to be friends only with Jewish people; it's just that we tend to gravitate toward those who are like ourselves.

Both my parents are Jewish, and they immersed me in the Jewish culture as a child. In Judaism, boys have a bar mitzvah at the age of 13, which is considered the age of accountability. They go through a ceremony at the Temple in which they read from the Torah (the first five books of the Bible). The word *bar* means son, and *mitzvah* means commandment. So when a boy reaches the age of 13, he accepts the responsibility to become a son of the commandments.

Most Jewish people today are secular; for them, Judaism is not so much a religion as it is an identity, culture, and way of life. It's like being Italian or Catholic for some people. Although they identify themselves with the culture, it doesn't necessarily define their beliefs. With many Jewish people, it is very important to be identified with the Jewish culture, but it doesn't necessarily define their belief in God.

Even though most Jewish men go through a bar mitzvah, oftentimes, afterwards they stop attending synagogue on a regular basis. You may hear a Jewish person say, "I'm Jewish from the top of my head to the bottom of my feet," but to them, being Jewish doesn't mean having a relationship with God. It's just a cultural identity and a connection to the Jewish community.

There are basically three branches of Judaism: Orthodox, Conservative, and Reform.

1. **Orthodox**: The orthodox branch strictly observes the Torah given to Moses at Mt. Sinai.
2. **Conservative**: The conservative branch maintains the ideas in the Torah as coming from God, but it believes the Law should adapt to the culture while remaining true to Judaic values.
3. **Reform**: The reform branch is the most liberal of the three branches. It doesn't accept the binding nature of the Law, but instead maintains a strong emphasis on social causes and doing good works.

My bar mitzvah, at the age of 13, was in a conservative Temple. In preparation for my bar mitzvah, I attended Hebrew school three times a week. The focus of my training was memorization of prayers, learning traditions, and reading Hebrew. I was never taught that I could have a personal relationship with God. My experience is not unique. Many temples do not teach the Jewish people that they can have a personal relationship with God. Their focus, basically, is tradition and reading Hebrew. You will find a high population of Jewish people in cults, because their hunger for God often isn't satisfied through traditional Jewish education.

Not long ago, one of my family members attended Temple, and as she spoke from the pulpit about having a relationship with God, she was rebuked by the rabbi, who told her that Jews cannot intimately know God; they can only follow His commandments. As a result of this Jewish mindset, my Hebrew school experience was devoid of nurturing a personal relationship with God.

TEENAGE YEARS

Growing up, I knew nothing about Jesus. I had received no Christian testimony or witness whatsoever in my life. When I was in seventh grade, my family moved to a very wealthy area of Cleveland called Pepper Pike that had a large Jewish population, but it wasn't entirely Jewish. Again, all my close friends were Jews, except for one Italian friend. He wore a big cross around his neck. Now, you might think he must have been the person that God used to bring the Gospel message to me, but that isn't what happened. He wore the cross around his neck, not because he was a Christian, but because the cross was an important symbol to him as an Italian. He was one of the toughest boys in school, and I used to follow him around just to watch him beat up other kids.

At the age of 13, I decided to get involved in the sport of wrestling. I had a cousin who wrestled, and I admired him. When you're 5'6", like me, you don't have aspirations of becoming a great basketball or football star. By the time I reached ninth grade, I was a pretty good wrestler. Wrestling became my identity. I was known as Kirt Schneider, the wrestler. Around my neck, I wore a necklace with an image of a wrestler. I defined myself as a wrestler, and my goal was to become the Ohio State high school wrestling champion in my weight class.

Wrestling became so important to me that every night, as I was getting ready to go to sleep, I would turn the record player on and listen to the song *Southern Man* by Crosby, Stills, Nash, and Young. As I would lie in bed listening to the music, I would envision myself with my hand raised as state champion. As I did that, chills would go through my body. In my young mind, becoming state champion would be like conquering the world. I believed, once I had won, I would spend the rest of my life basking in the sunshine of my victory. I would celebrate the glory of it, and the rest of my life would be a piece of cake.

Up to this point in my life, I truly never thought of life beyond wrestling. All I thought about was becoming state champion, but when I walked off the wrestling mat after my last match as a high school senior, it was as if my world had been pulled out instantaneously from under my feet. Suddenly, I realized I would be entering a world that was much bigger than people who wrestled 119 pounds and that wrestling didn't mean much in the real world. I lost my identity and purpose in life, and I went from believing that I was on top of the world, to feeling very small. I was completely lost, and it was absolutely terrifying.

COLLEGE YEARS

Although I never became state champion, I did receive a small college wrestling scholarship to the University of Tampa. My grades were okay, but I still continued to suffer and struggle with my loss of identity and purpose. I spent as much time as possible sleeping just to escape the mental and emotional pain. Nothing excited me anymore. I longed for that feeling of contentment, the sense of power and control, and the identity and purpose that wrestling had given me during my high school years.

As I contemplated my future, I considered becoming a doctor, but I knew I didn't possess the needed aptitude. I also considered becoming a lawyer, because I had good communication skills. I thought to myself, "I could be Kirt Schneider, the lawyer," but then I considered, "What would happen if I became a successful lawyer and the time came when I would have to retire? Would I feel as lost as I did when wrestling ended?" I couldn't get excited about becoming a lawyer, because I knew my life would be built on something, once again, that would eventually end, and I didn't want that to happen. I needed something in my life that would be permanent.

Yeshua spoke about building our lives on something permanent. He illustrated this principle by comparing two people: one who built his house on the Rock and the other who built his house on the sand.

> [24]*"Therefore everyone who hears these words of mine and puts them into practice is like a wise man who built his house on the rock.* [25]*The rain came down, the streams rose, and the winds blew and beat against that house; yet it did not fall, because it had its foundation on the rock.* [26]*But everyone who hears these words of mine and does not put them into practice is like a foolish man who built his house on sand.* [27]*The rain came down, the streams rose, and the winds blew and beat against that house, and it fell with a great crash."*
> *-Matthew 7:24-27 NIV*

When the wind and waves came, the person's house built on the Rock stood firm, but the person's house built on the sand stood firm for only awhile, and then its foundation was washed away. If you are to stand firm when the wind and waves of life come against you, then you must build your life on a firm foundation. That foundation is Yeshua, the Rock of life.

Of course, I didn't know my thoughts, at the time, were based on the words of Yeshua; I just knew I didn't want my life built on something that would get washed away again. I needed something in my life I could count on, but I had no idea what it would be or where I would find it. I hadn't thought of God as the answer, because my experience growing up in the synagogue didn't nurture or teach me about having a personal relationship with Him.

During this phase of my life, I believed if I became financially successful, it would help ease my pain and make me feel better about myself. Frankly, I knew wealth wasn't the answer. After all, I had grown up in an affluent neighborhood, and I observed that wealthy people still had problems like anyone else. They may not have had the same problems, but they still had problems. Even though I knew money didn't guarantee happiness and wouldn't solve my problems, I didn't know what else to do, so I dropped out of college in my second year to pursue the goal of becoming financially successful by opening a discotheque.

EARLY ADULT YEARS

It was 1978, and discos were really hot. Some may remember John Travolta dancing in *Saturday Night Fever* under the crystal disco ball. People stood in lines a quarter mile long in Cleveland to get into a discotheque. I figured if I could start a disco in a fairly large community that didn't already have one, they would line up at the doors to get in.

To open the discotheque, I would need financing, and my plan was to obtain the necessary finances through friends of our family, who lived in the neighborhood. Once the finances were obtained, I would be part owner and be in charge of running the business. The main obstacle I encountered was securing investors. No one would invest in the disco, because they said I didn't have a solid business plan.

I then got a job selling encyclopedias door-to-door, simply to make money, so I could travel throughout the Midwest, finding the perfect location for my discotheque. I knew finding the right location would be the key to having a solid business plan.

I did fairly well selling encyclopedias; at the same time, I continued researching my disco venture. As I continued researching, I came to the realization that I lacked the necessary business knowledge and savvy to be successful at starting a discotheque, so I continued selling encyclopedias as I contemplated my future.

Eventually, I was promoted to sales manager and was given a team of people to train. One evening, I went to a meeting where six sales managers were to be in attendance. When I arrived, there was only one other sales manager there. As he and I waited for the others to arrive, he began to tell me about a book he had been reading called *Autobiography of a Yogi*. It sounded fascinating to me! He told me there was a yogi from India that could beat up tigers with his bare hands. I was so intrigued by the fantastic feats he said the yogi performed, that I went and bought the book. It was the first book I ever bought with my own money.

As I read the book, I was fascinated with all the miraculous and supernatural things this yogi claimed to do. There were pictures of him, supposedly levitating supernaturally off the ground. I didn't know if the pictures were done with trick photography or whether he really was levitating off the ground.

As I continued to be in awe of the pictures, I said, "God, if this is real, if he can really levitate off the ground, this is what I want to do with the rest of my life." Even though I did not have a faith that was established by any specific set of doctrines, I still had a strong faith that there was a God, even from childhood. I said to myself, "I will spend the rest of my life doing whatever I need to do, so I can get to the place where I can levitate off the ground. This will be my new wrestling." I knew if I could just levitate off the ground, I would have tremendous bliss in my life. This now became the focus of my life and a higher reality than making money.

OVERCOMING SPIRITUAL DARKNESS

One summer night in 1978, the LORD put a stop to my searching for the miraculous and supernatural in *Autobiography of a Yogi*. As I slept in my bed that night at Bremerton Road in Pepper Pike, Ohio, the LORD awoke me from my sleep. Even though my eyes were closed, I was aware I wasn't sleeping. I was in a state of conscious awareness, and it was as if I was being translated into another realm. I had not been taking drugs nor was I drunk.

In an instant, Jesus Christ (Yeshua HaMashiach) appeared on the cross. The terrain was in color, and there were people in the distance looking at Him. Suddenly, a ray of red light from the sky beamed straight down on His head. I knew it was coming from God, since it was coming from above.

I had never experienced a vision before and never even thought about what a vision was, but I knew, somehow, that God had just revealed Himself to me and had shown me that Jesus (Yeshua) was the way to Him. No one had ever witnessed to me about Jesus, and I had never read the New Testament. As a Jew, I had been taught that Jesus was not for Jews, but as an American, I knew enough to know the person on the cross was Jesus.

When the vision ended, I got out of bed and looked at my clock radio. It was 3:30 in the morning. Again, I had never considered what a vision was, but I somehow knew I had just experienced a vision. Even though it only lasted a few seconds, I was so excited. I was 20 years old and had been so lost, searching for meaning and purpose in my life and trying to escape my fears. Now God had revealed Himself to me, showing me the answer!

As time went on, I came to realize that God had literally translated me 2,000 years back in time to visibly witness Yeshua being crucified. I came to this understanding while reading Luke 23:49, which describes the people who were watching Him being crucified from "a distance." In my vision, I specifically saw, not only the color of the terrain in which the cross was staked, but also the people who were watching His crucifixion from "a distance."

> [49]*But all those who knew him, including the women who had followed him from Galilee, stood at a distance, watching these things. ~Luke 23:49 NIV*

Since I had never been exposed to faith in Jesus, I didn't understand how He was the way to God, but eventually God would show me. In my excitement, I started telling everyone about the vision. Later, someone told me I should buy a New Testament. I did, and I started devouring it. It was like fire to me. As I read it, I realized the teaching was different from the book, *Autobiography of a Yogi,* so I threw away the *Autobiography of a Yogi* and continued reading the New Testament. Praise God!

I realized the victory I had sought in life through wrestling is found in Yeshua. I started overcoming the spiritual darkness in my life, and as I pressed on in Him, I was continually strengthened. I began to ascend out of the darkness and into the light. I still have a long way to go, but He became my source of life, a river of living water in me.

> [13]*Jesus answered, "Everyone who drinks this water will be thirsty again,* [14]*but whoever drinks the water I give him will never thirst. Indeed, the water I give him will become in him a spring of water welling up to eternal life." ~John 4:13-14 NIV*

Those of us who press on in Yeshua will be strengthened and will ascend to new heights by His Spirit. The spiritual darkness over our lives will break up, and one day we will be sitting on the clouds of glory with Yeshua HaMashiach, the King of glory, and we will reign with Him forever and ever and ever.

INITIAL REJECTION

On the morning I received the vision of Yeshua, I was so excited that God had revealed Himself to me that I started telling my entire family about the vision. Aside from my mom and dad, I have a brother who is one year younger and a sister who is four years younger. In my initial excitement and naivety, I believed they would be as excited as I was. I couldn't perceive Yeshua from any other point of view but my own.

My parents had faced anti-Semitism growing up, something I had never encountered. For this reason, I had no concept of what I would experience when I began to tell them about Jesus. At first, they didn't react much. They probably figured it was only a dream and my excitement would subside in a couple of days. Instead, I started telling everyone about Jesus. I started pointing out certain Bible verses to my dad. Again, in my ignorance, I thought he would be as excited as I was. I was so eager and hungry to learn more about Jesus that I began attending churches throughout the city of Cleveland.

My parents were stricken with panic. In their minds, it was a shameful and terrible thing to have their son running all over the place talking about Jesus. Although Yeshua proclaimed that all men will know His followers by their love, what the Jewish people have experienced from the Christian community is hatred and persecution, not love. Now their Jewish son was walking around their Jewish neighborhood telling all the neighbors about Jesus. I was a traitor to the Jewish community, a shameful and hard thing for my family to bear.

DEPROGRAMMING EXPERIENCE

When my parents realized how serious I was about Yeshua and that it wasn't a passing phase, they hired the most famous deprogrammer in the country to kidnap and deprogram me. One day my dad invited me to go with him to a hotel to talk to a gentleman about opening a restaurant. My dad said, "Maybe we'll be in business together. Come with me to discuss opening a restaurant."

That Sunday we drove to a hotel in the Beachwood area of Cleveland. As we walked into the hotel room, there were three people in the room. There was a short, distinguished-looking gentleman dressed in a three-piece suit, who was in his 50s, and there were two other men, both over six feet tall and 200 pounds.

After we walked into the room, the door closed behind us, and the short distinguished-looking man, who I later found out was the head deprogrammer, said to me, "Kirt, we're going to talk about cults." Immediately, he turned on a projector that had been set up in the room, and he showed me a video about Hare Krishnas. He pointed to a four-year-old child in the movie and said, "You see that kid? There's nothing I can do for him. All he's known is Hare Krishna, and I can't snap him out of it."

He said to me, "You've been living for 20 years as a normal person, but now you're constantly talking about Jesus, giving all your money to the church, and reading the most dangerous book in the world, the Bible. I'm going to snap you out of this."

I said to him, "I'm not programmed by anyone; I just believe that Yeshua is the Messiah." He said, "Then you've got nothing to worry about." I asked him, "Can I leave?" One of the big men said, "Sit down!"

I was trapped in the room. They allowed me to go to the bathroom, and I got down on my knees with my face on the floor, and I prayed, "LORD, I don't know what's ahead of me or what I'm about to go through, but please keep me as I go through it."

We eventually left the hotel room, and one of the big men accompanied me to our house. He stayed with me continuously, even sleeping in my bedroom that night, so I couldn't get away. The next day I was taken to a rehabilitation house in California. I was there for two weeks. At the time, I felt bad for my parents, because I'm sure it cost them a lot of money.

The rehabilitation house was run by the deprogrammer's son. My rehabilitation consisted of being taken every day to the beach during the day and to the bars at night. After two weeks of this, I was then allowed to go back home. The deprogrammers and my parents had hoped that by getting me away from the environment that they believed was programming me to follow Jesus, I would snap out of it and come back to my senses.

Obviously, my faith in Yeshua was not rooted in someone programming me. It was rooted in a personal, supernatural revelation from the Father, so it couldn't be shaken. My faith was built on a personal revelation from the LORD just like Peter's (Kepha's).

> [13]*When Jesus came to the region of Caesarea Philippi, he asked his disciples, "Who do people say the Son of Man is?"* [14]*They replied, "Some say John the Baptist; others say Elijah; and still others, Jeremiah or one of the prophets."* [15]*"But what about you?" he asked. "Who do you say I am?"* [16]*Simon Peter answered, "You are the (Messiah), the Son of the living God."* [17]*Jesus replied, "Blessed are you, Simon son of Jonah, for this was not revealed to you by man, but by my Father in heaven." ~Matthew 16:13-17 NIV*

PSYCHIATRIC WARD EXPERIENCE

When I got back home from the deprogramming experience, I decided I needed to be a little less vocal about my faith. Apparently, I wasn't less vocal enough, because not long afterwards, my parents hired a psychiatrist to come to the house to evaluate me. The psychiatrist was a very short, frail, sickly-looking man with balding red hair. My parents and I sat down with him at the dining room table, and he started asking me questions.

I began telling him how Yeshua had appeared to me in a vision. I testified of Yeshua's greatness and of all the things He had done for me. I also explained what my life would be like if Yeshua hadn't delivered me. The psychiatrist sat there quietly listening, not saying a word, and after an hour he left.

After he left, I went to see one of my Christian friends. I don't say this proudly, because I was very young and immature, but I told my friend how I had made mincemeat out of the psychiatrist. I boasted of how I boldly witnessed to him about Yeshua.

Later, I realized the psychiatrist was actually baiting me. He wanted me to tell him about my vision of Yeshua, so he could diagnosis me as delusional and have me committed to a psychiatric ward. This was the reason my parents had hired him. They were hopeful I could be treated by a psychiatrist, come to my senses, and renounce my faith in Yeshua.

The psychiatrist went through the court system and was successful in committing me to a hospital psychiatric ward. Now, here I was, a young man in my twenties, locked up with absolutely no place to go and nothing to do. I woke up every morning full of energy, with no way to release it, and each day became increasingly more difficult to handle. Before this had happened, I had come to a point in my life where I was starting to feel good again. I had started a new life for myself, building it in Yeshua, but now here I was, locked up, basically imprisoned for my belief in Him.

After a few days, I was placed in a group therapy session. There was a lady in this group, who was having a difficult time coping with the loss of her husband, who had recently passed away. She started telling the group how her late husband was the most wonderful man who had ever lived and how he was now in heaven. I asked her if he had known Jesus, and she replied, "No, we're both Jewish." I said to her, in a less than tactful manner, "If he didn't know Jesus, he isn't in heaven. It's heaven with Jesus or hell without Him."

After I told her that, I was told I would be placed on medication to control my behavior, because I was disturbing the equilibrium of the group. I was also informed that if I didn't voluntarily take the medication, I would be strapped down and injected with it, so I decided to take it "voluntarily." The medication made me feel very uncomfortable. Because I had so much energy trapped inside me, with no way to release it, every time I sat down in a chair, my legs would continuously bob up and down.

At the time, there was a state law that stated if a psychiatrist probated you to a psychiatric ward, you had to stay there for a period of two months, and then a court hearing would be held to determine if you needed to stay. Well, after two months, I was interviewed by a team of psychiatrists, and they recognized that I didn't need to be there, so I was released.

PERSECUTION FOR MY FAITH IN YESHUA

After being released from the psychiatric ward, it took me several months to begin to recuperate and get back on my feet. God, in His faithfulness, strengthened me and led me onward and upward. I continued being less vocal about Yeshua, but difficulties and problems still persisted. I ended up being thrown out of my parent's house, and I lost all my friends. Although all these things happened, I found comfort in what Yeshua promised to those who are persecuted for His sake.

> [29]*"I tell you the truth," Jesus replied, "no one who has left home or brothers or sisters or mother or father or children or fields for me and the gospel* [30]*will fail to receive a hundred times as much in this present age (homes, brothers, sisters, mothers, children and fields—and with them, persecutions) and in the age to come, eternal life." ~Mark 10:29-30 NIV*

> [10]*"Blessed are those who are persecuted because of righteousness, for theirs is the kingdom of heaven.* [11]*Blessed are you when people insult you, persecute you and falsely say all kinds of evil against you because of me.* [12]*Rejoice and be glad, because great is your reward in heaven, for in the same way they persecuted the prophets who were before you." ~Matthew 5:10-12 NIV*

My faith in Yeshua has continued to create struggles and division in our family throughout the years. One example of this is when my niece had her bat mitzvah, the Jewish female version of a boy's bar mitzvah. They had a special ceremony for her, but I was not invited to participate because of my faith in Yeshua.

Yeshua told His followers that because He chose them out of the world, they were not of the world, and the world would hate them.

> [19]*"If you belonged to the world, it would love you as its own. As it is, you do not belong to the world, but I have chosen you out of the world. That is why the world hates you." ~John 15:19 NIV*

Yeshua also told His followers that a servant isn't greater than his master; if He was persecuted, they also would be persecuted.

> [20]*"Remember the words I spoke to you: 'No servant is greater than his master. If they persecuted me, they will persecute you also.'" ~John 15:20a NIV*

Since receiving the supernatural vision of Yeshua from God in 1978, I have withstood tremendous rejection and hostility from the Jewish community for my faith, but my faith has never wavered. Don't ever shrink away from testifying of your faith in Yeshua to anyone. If you're rejected and suffer for Him, consider it a privilege. You'll be rewarded, and God will strengthen you, affirming your identity in Him. In fact, it has been appointed for us, not just to reign with Him, but to suffer with Him as well. We are called to fill up the sufferings of Messiah.

> [24] *Now I rejoice in my sufferings … in my flesh I do my share on behalf of His body, which is the church, in filling up what is lacking in (Messiah's) afflictions.* ~ *Colossians 1:24 NASB*

> [12] *If we suffer, we shall also reign with him: ~ 2 Timothy 2:12a KJV*

MY FAITH JOURNEY

After losing my family and friends, I decided there was nothing left for me in Cleveland. I therefore decided to leave everything behind and start my life over, just the LORD and I. I imagined being like Abraham, who left his home to follow God, not knowing where he was going.

> [1] *The LORD had said to Abram, "Leave your country, your people and your father's household and go to the land I will show you." ~ Genesis 12:1 NIV*

What I did next, I would not recommend to anyone, even though the LORD used it in my life. I took a map of the United States, laid it on the ground, and then closing my eyes, I flipped a coin, saying, "LORD, wherever this coin lands, that's where I'm going to go, just You and me. I'm not going to tell anyone where I'm going. I'm going to start my life over, just You and me."

When I flipped the coin, it landed on Park Rapids, Minnesota. The next day I packed up my orange AMC Gremlin and headed towards Park Rapids. I was elated! The LORD and I were starting over, just Him and I. I just knew it would be glorious! I even envisioned myself pastoring a church when I got there.

When I arrived in Park Rapids, I discovered it to be an Indian reservation. It was a ghost town; hardly anyone was even living there. The only job available in the whole town was working on a ski slope. I would have had to invest $200 in ski equipment and clothing to work there, and then the job wouldn't start for another two months. On top of that, I didn't even know how to ski.

At this point, I knew I couldn't stay in Park Rapids. I thought to myself, "What am I going to do?" I knew I had to get someplace warm, so when I ran out of money, I wouldn't freeze to death. I counted the money I had left in my wallet and calculated how many miles I could travel with that money. I looked at a map and figured I had just enough for one last meal and enough to get me to Corpus Christi, Texas. I had never been there before, but I assumed, "It must be warm, because it's on the ocean." Even though I'd be out of money when I arrived, I hoped it would be warm enough there to survive.

On the way to Corpus Christi, I stopped for my last meal at a restaurant in Kansas City, Missouri. After finishing the meal, I got back in my Gremlin, but it wouldn't start. Now I didn't have enough money to get my car fixed and get to Corpus Christi. I thought to myself, "What am I going to do?" I ended up giving my car to the waitress at the restaurant.

I then went into the restaurant's restroom and threw my wallet and glasses into the trash can and said, "LORD, I'm going to rely on You alone." I know this sounds unstable and radical, but God used this time in my life to teach me to trust and rely only upon Him. It became the grounding of my manhood in the LORD. I learned to be confident in Him, as I ventured out with nothing to rely on but Him.

Having given my car away, I needed a change of plans. I decided to head to California, where I would fast in the northern woods. I started hitchhiking. The first two days, no one picked me up. The first night, I slept on the side of the road in the weeds. The next night, I slept on a bench in an all-night sports coliseum. Those were very lonely days.

On the third day, someone finally offered me a ride; however, he wasn't going to California, but was on his way to Amarillo, Texas, to visit a friend. He told me that his friend owned a Tex-Mex restaurant, and he would give me a job working there. When I got to Amarillo, I started working at the restaurant as a line cook. I ran into difficulty, because I was having trouble seeing, since I had thrown away my glasses in Kansas City. The orders were spun around on a wheel, and I couldn't see them without walking from one end of the kitchen, back to the wheel on the other side of the kitchen. This considerably slowed down the production line. Eventually, I ended up getting released from the job because of my vision problems.

From there, I did end up going to California. I lived with one of my relatives and worked as a graveyard dishwasher in a Sambo's Restaurant. I had left home to seek the LORD, believing it would be a glorious experience, but now here I was, two months later, working in a restaurant as a graveyard dishwasher. I had no car, and I was riding my little cousin's bicycle to work every day, while my brother and sister were on their way to success. I began to feel like a real loser, because the Jewish community tends to be very focused on education, with many becoming doctors, lawyers, or successful business owners. Here I was, without a college degree, working as a graveyard dishwasher, riding my little cousin's bicycle to work. It felt like I was on the road to nowhere.

I said, "LORD, I really am beginning to feel bad about myself. If I ever make $100,000 in a single year, it will be a miracle!" It wasn't that I was seeking riches; I just wanted to feel better about myself and was measuring myself by the affluent Jewish community that I had grown up in. It was only a few years after praying this prayer to God that He put me in a position where I made $111,000 in one year. The LORD is awesome! I'm not bragging about how much I made, since all that money meant nothing to me. I'm just testifying to the goodness and lovingkindness of my Father God.

MARRIAGE AND BIBLE COLLEGE

Eventually, the LORD brought me back home to Cleveland. The journey He had taken me on shaped me into a new man. It's like one who enlists in the Marines and after finishing boot camp is a new person, because they've been through an experience that has imparted something within. The LORD used my experiences to impart His strength within me and build a strong faith and trust in Him.

After returning to Cleveland, it wasn't long before many things in my life started changing. Within a month, I met my future wife, Cynthia, who also became a follower of Jesus. We were married in 1983. Bringing Cynthia into my life was the LORD's way of straightening me out and getting me on track in many ways. Without her love and influence in my life, I would not be where I am today.

I also enrolled in Toccoa Falls, a fully accredited Bible college. This college was very good for me; I learned a great many things, and I truly enjoyed my time there. Looking back on those days, I am thankful that they didn't throw me out of this Bible college. Almost all of the students attending there had come from Christian homes, and they knew what was acceptable or unacceptable behavior in a Christian setting. As for me, I came right out of the world, and looking back, I cringe at some of the things that came out of my mouth, not knowing any better. One professor told me that he thought I was like Peter, "a diamond in the rough." I believe that they put up with me, because I was Jewish, and they saw potential in me.

Although this college was very strong and committed to most aspects of the Word of God, they discouraged seeking the supernatural and many types of ministry associated with the spiritual gifts. I recall one student from Bible college who was very charismatic. One evening I invited him and his wife to my home to have dinner with Cynthia and I. As the evening went on, he began sharing with us how he was able to speak in tongues, something I had never done. In fact, one of my professors had us listen to a cassette tape, in which an evangelist cast a demon out of someone, whom the professor claimed came in when this individual sought to speak in tongues. As a result, I was afraid to seek this gift.

Now, here was a fellow student and friend telling me he had spoken in tongues. As he was speaking to me about the fact that God gives believers this gift as a prayer language, the LORD clearly bore witness with my spirit that this friend was telling me the truth. It was shocking to me that at the very instant God's Spirit was bearing witness to me that what my friend was telling me was the truth, my friend said to me, "What are you feeling right now?" I am ashamed to say that I said, "Oh, I'm not feeling anything." I covered up the truth and suppressed the witness of the Holy Spirit within me.

It's been many years since then, and now God has released me into a much fuller walk with the Holy Spirit, including all the gifts of the Spirit, but I'll never forget that moment. The LORD had clearly spoken to me, and I'm so ashamed to think back on how I suppressed His Spirit. My hope is that you won't suppress God's Spirit in your life. The

LORD wants to lead you into a richer and fuller experience of His Ruach HaKodesh (Holy Spirit).

STARTING INTO MINISTRY

When I graduated from Toccoa Falls College in 1985, I was awarded "The Preacher of the Year Award." The award was a blessing from God, because it opened up doors in ministry for me.

I began ministering in 1985 in a mainline denomination. I found my position very difficult to cope with, because everything done in this congregation was by congregational vote. I had to contend with church politics and all the tradition and culture that had been there prior to my arrival. Being young and immature, I found it very difficult to handle. After all, I still had a lot of issues in my own life that needed to be resolved. For personal reasons, I decided to take a sabbatical from ministry.

SABBATICAL FROM MINISTRY

During my sabbatical from ministry, I worked in the business world in sales and motivational speaking. I started out in the area of insurance and investments. In the first year, I won a national sales contest, competing against other new agents, but I found it difficult to earn a good living.

From there, I began selling new residential homes, and I was the number one salesperson in the last company I worked for. During my years as a salesperson, I observed that many in the sales field did a very good job explaining their product, but they were afraid to ask for the sale. If they'd only had the courage to overcome their fears, their sales would have increased.

I decided to start giving motivational talks to sales representatives to help them overcome their fears. In preparation, I did extensive research on the topic of fear. I ultimately knew the cause of fear was Satan and darkness, but I wanted to see what had been written by others and what studies had been done.

Although there were several theories on the origin of fear, there was nothing written on solutions for fear. I asked myself, "How have I overcome fear?" Instantly, I knew the answer. It was Yeshua! It was a eureka moment; immediately I knew I had to get out of business and back into ministry. The message I had to share was the message of Yeshua!

RETURN TO MINISTRY

I started back into ministry, and the LORD quickly and supernaturally opened many doors for me. He led me to start a traveling ministry called Shalom Ministries International, in which I minister to churches on the Jewish roots of our faith in Yeshua. Through this ministry, I spoke several times at Adat Adonai Messianic Synagogue (Hebrew for the "Congregation of the LORD"), which is now located in Ottawa Lake, Michigan. Through this connection, they asked me to become their rabbi. The LORD then opened the door for me to start a weekly television program, *Discovering the Jewish Jesus*, which, as of this writing, is being broadcast throughout the world, even into Israel.

Chapter Two

Messiah In You, The Hope of Glory

MESSIAH IN YOU

Within this chapter, I will lay a scriptural foundation to help you become more aware of the reality that Yeshua the Messiah lives inside all born again believers through the Ruach HaKodesh (Hebrew for the Holy Spirit). After laying a scriptural foundation, I will share several of my own personal experiences in which I have personally encountered the Spirit of God. In sharing these experiences, I hope to help you grasp the reality that the Ruach HaKodesh is real and that He lives in you. Next, I will present several practical life applications which will help you to develop a greater spiritual sensitivity and awareness of God's Spirit within you. Lastly, I will share several action steps you can take to help you cultivate greater intimacy with God in your life.

THE NEW COVENANT

In the Hebrew Bible (Old Testament), Yahweh dealt with mankind mostly from the outside. He wrote His Law (the Ten Commandments) on the tablets of stone, and when Israel wanted to meet with Him, they had to meet Him in a specific place, such as the Tabernacle or the Temple in Jerusalem.

The Hebrew prophets foretold of Yahweh making a New Covenant (B'rit Chadashah) with Israel. This New Covenant would not be like the Old Covenant given to their forefathers; it would be entirely new. Yahweh would move His presence from the outside to the inside by placing His Law and His Spirit within us.

[31]*"The time is coming," declares the LORD, "when I will make a new covenant with the house of Israel and with the house of Judah.* [32] *It will not be like the covenant I made with their forefathers when I took them by the hand to lead them out of Egypt, because they broke my covenant, though I was a husband to them," declares the LORD.* [33]*"This is the covenant I will make with the house of Israel after that time," declares the LORD. "I will put my law in their minds and write it on their hearts. I will be their God, and they will be my people.* [34]*No longer will a man teach his neighbor, or a man his brother, saying, 'Know the LORD,' because they will all know me, from the least of them to the greatest," declares the LORD. -Jeremiah 31:31-34a NIV*

[26]*"I will give you a new heart and put a new spirit in you; I will remove from you your heart of stone (hard heart) and give you a heart of flesh (sensitive heart).* [27]*And I will put my Spirit in you and move you to*

follow my decrees and be careful to keep my laws."
~Ezekiel 36:26-27 NIV

This New Covenant is fulfilled in Yeshua, and it is based on two primary foundations:
1. Final atonement for sin has been made.
2. The Ruach HaKodesh has been placed within believers.

1. FINAL ATONEMENT FOR SIN

The Hebrew Bible describes how Yahweh required a blood sacrifice of an unblemished animal for the atonement of Israel's sin. These sacrifices needed to be offered day after day and year after year, because the blood sacrifices of bulls and goats never really took away sin.

> [4]*"because it is impossible for the blood of bulls and goats to take away sins." ~Hebrews 10:4 NIV*

These sacrifices were simply shadows of the one ultimate sacrifice, Yeshua, who in offering Himself up as a sacrifice for sin, took away the need to ever offer sacrifices again. In other words, the sacrifices offered in the Tabernacle and later in the Temple, under the Levitical Priesthood, were shadows of the real payment that was to come. The real payment was God, Himself, who came to earth in the flesh as Yeshua.

It is Yeshua who fulfilled the Levitical sacrificial system. He is the innocent, sinless One, who died in our place for the forgiveness of our sin: past, present, and future. Through Him, all our sins have been forgiven, once and for all, eliminating the need for any further sacrifices.

2. THE PLACING OF THE
RUACH HAKODESH IN BELIEVERS

The second foundation of the New Covenant is the gift of the Ruach HaKodesh to believers. In the Hebrew Bible, God gave His Spirit to only a few priests and kings, but with the inauguration of the New Covenant, God's Spirit would be poured out on all flesh: sons and daughters, old and young, whomever received Yeshua. This pouring out of God's Spirit was prophesied by the Hebrew prophet, Joel (Yo'el).

> [28]*"And afterward, I will pour out my Spirit on all people. Your sons and daughters will prophesy, your old men will dream dreams, your young men will see visions.* [29]*Even on my servants, both men and women, I will pour out my Spirit in those days." -Joel 2:28-29 NIV*

Now through Yeshua, all are invited to come to Him and become recipients of His Spirit.

THE NEW COVENANT
INAUGURATED AT PASSOVER

Yeshua instituted this New Covenant when He celebrated Passover with His disciples before He was crucified. As He lifted up the Passover wine, He proclaimed that His shed blood would establish the basis on which the New Covenant is founded.

> [27]*Then he took the cup, gave thanks and offered it to them, saying, "Drink from it, all of you.* [28]*This is my blood of the covenant, which is poured out for many for the forgiveness of sins." -Matthew 26:27-28 NIV*

THE PROMISE OF THE RUACH HAKODESH

Yeshua explained to His disciples that the Ruach HaKodesh had been with them and would later be in them.

> [16]*"And I will ask the Father, and he will give you another Counselor to be with you forever—* [17]*the Spirit of truth. The world cannot accept him, because it neither sees him nor knows him. But you know him, for he lives with you and will be in you." -John 14:16-17 NIV*

Yeshua would literally live inside each born again believer through the Spirit of God. Before ascending to heaven, He instructed His disciples to stay in Jerusalem until they received the promise of the Ruach HaKodesh.

> [49]*"I am going to send you what my Father has promised; but stay in the city until you have been clothed with power from on high." -Luke 24:49 NIV*

THE RUACH HAKODESH GIVEN

As recorded in the second chapter of Acts, Yeshua's followers were in Jerusalem celebrating the feast of Shavuot (the Hebrew name for Pentecost). They were celebrating what Yahweh had done 1500 years earlier, when He appeared to the children of Israel on Mt. Sinai with fire and glory, giving them the two tablets of stone (The Ten Commandments).

As they were celebrating, suddenly a rushing, violent wind filled the house where they were gathered, and they were instantly filled with the Ruach HaKodesh. What had formally been written on tablets of stone, now was written on their hearts by the Spirit of God.

They began boldly proclaiming the mighty acts of God by speaking in languages they didn't know, because the Spirit of power and life literally came inside them. Many who witnessed what was happening were bewildered and amazed, while others accused them of being drunk. Peter (Kefa) stood up and declared that they were not drunk, since it was only the third hour of the day. He proclaimed that what they had just witnessed had been prophesied by the prophet Joel (Yo'el).

Yahweh was literally indwelling believers with His Spirit of power and life; they now had become the temple of the Ruach HaKodesh.

> [16]*"Don't you know that you yourselves are God's temple and that God's Spirit lives in you?" ~1 Corinthians 3:16 NIV*

THE REALITY OF GOD'S SPIRIT WITHIN US

The reality of God's Spirit, literally dwelling within us, is a difficult concept for many of us to grasp. Many believers have a difficult time laying hold of the reality that Jesus lives inside them, because the western culture of Christianity has taken the mystical aspect of walking with God out of our faith. The apostle Paul (Shaul) said that he had been made a minister of a mystery, and that mystery is "Messiah in you."

> [26]*"the mystery that has been kept hidden for ages and generations, but is now disclosed to the saints. [27]To them God has chosen to make known among the Gentiles the glorious riches of this mystery, which is (Messiah) in you, the hope of glory." ~Colossians 1:26-27 NIV*

Shaul learned how to be led by the indwelling Ruach HaKodesh. We have become so scientific and logical in our culture that we have lost a connection with the mystical. The secularism of today's culture, manifesting through our media and entertainment, causes us to place our emphasis outside of ourselves. When this happens, we lose touch with what is within. When we seek to find God outside ourselves, we fail to find Him, because He's not on the outside; He's within us.

Yeshua explained to the Pharisees of His day that the Kingdom of God wasn't "here or there," where one could see it, but it was within.

> [20] *Once, having been asked by the Pharisees when the kingdom of God would come, Jesus replied, "The kingdom of God does not come with your careful observation,* [21] *nor will people say, 'Here it is,' or 'There it is,' because the kingdom of God is within you." -Luke 17:20-21 NIV*

THE MYSTERY OF THE AGES

The mystery of the ages is Messiah in you, the hope of glory. This mystery of God living within us goes all the way back to the beginning of time with the first man, Adam.

> [45] *"So it is written: 'The first man Adam became a living being'; the last Adam, a life-giving spirit.* [46] *The spiritual did not come first, but the natural, and after that the spiritual.* [47] *The first man was of the dust of the earth, the second man from heaven." -1 Corinthians 15:45-47 NIV*

The first man, Adam, was a living soul, but the last Adam, who is Yeshua, is a life-giving spirit. The first Adam was natural, while the last Adam is spiritual.

I believe the fall of mankind was actually part of the design of Yahweh, Himself. If the first Adam had never fallen, none of us would be born again with God's Spirit living within us. The first Adam lived in God's presence, but he wasn't born again. He never had God's Spirit as his own personal possession (Ephesians 1:14). He wasn't a child of God in the same way as those who have literally become "partakers of the divine nature" of God (2 Peter 1:4). Because the first Adam fell, the last Adam came and redeemed us, putting His Spirit within us; we are now called the sons of God. We now have a higher place than the first Adam. We literally have God's Spirit inhabiting us, something Adam never had.

So we see from the very beginning that God had a plan to make us partakers of His Spirit and divine nature. This happens through spiritual rebirth. We are born into this world with a human nature through our biological parents, but in order to receive a second nature, God's nature, we must be born again.

> [3]*Jesus declared, "I tell you the truth, no one can see the kingdom of God unless he is born again." -John 3:3b NIV*

When we speak of being born again, we are not speaking of some philosophy or turning over a new leaf in life. Being born again isn't just a doctrine of belief; it is a scientific spiritual reality. God literally places His Spirit inside His children.

When those first followers of Yeshua spoke in languages they didn't know on Shavuot (Pentecost), it happened because there was a life force (the Holy Spirit) within them uttering those words. That same life force caused Yeshua to ascend from earth to heaven, and if you are born again, it lives in you.

> [8]*"But you will receive power when the Holy Spirit comes on you; and you will be my witnesses in Jerusalem, and in all Judea and Samaria, and to the ends of the earth."* [9]*After he said this, he was taken up before their very eyes, and a cloud hid him from their sight. ~Acts 1:8-9 NIV*

SEEING INTO THE SPIRIT REALM

From the time Yeshua supernaturally revealed Himself to me in 1978, my desire has been to continuously walk with an awareness of God's supernatural presence in my life. Approximately a year after receiving the vision of Yeshua on the cross, I experienced another major spiritual encounter. This encounter was similar to the one the apostle Shaul experienced that he couldn't fully explain.

> [1]*"I will go on to visions and revelations from the Lord.* [2]*I know a man in (Messiah) who fourteen years ago was caught up to the third heaven. Whether it was in the body or out of the body I do not know—God knows." ~2 Corinthians 12:1b-2 NIV*

The reason I share this verse with you is because the experience I'm about to share with you is not a typical vision or dream. Like the apostle Shaul, who described his encounter by saying he didn't know "whether it was in the body or out of the body," so, too, the experience I'm about to describe, I cannot fully explain. What I do know is that

God opened up the spirit realm to me and allowed me to see into the spirit world.

One night while I was sleeping, God actually allowed me to see spirit. What I saw had nothing to do with what I had for dinner nor did it have anything to do with what happened to me that day. What God allowed me to see that night was way beyond anything the human mind could ever create or fabricate.

That night I literally saw two spirits. The first spirit was shaped like an egg. It was sealed and self-contained and appeared to be two and a half to three feet long by approximately a foot and a half wide. Every part of this sealed, self-contained spirit was in constant motion, bubbling up with pure, white, eternal life. The spirit moved in perfect coordination, and its motion reminded me of a friend of mine in high school who was the best dancer in the school. When he danced, he was so coordinated that his dancing was art in motion; likewise, this sealed, self-contained spirit of pure, white life was alive and moving with perfect grace.

This spirit of white life was entirely surrounded by darkness, and this darkness was much more than the absence of light. This spirit of darkness was also alive and in motion, like the spirit of life, except it moved in a totally different way. While the spirit of life moved with complete coordination, the spirit of darkness moved in a chaotic motion. This spirit of darkness had a radically different type of life force from that of the spirit of life. In other words, the spirits of darkness and life were both alive, but they had completely different life forces.

We live in a spiritual world comprised of both the spirit of light and life, and the spirit of darkness and death. The spirit of light and life is Yeshua. The light of His Spirit shines through the darkness, and the darkness will never be able to extinguish it.

> ⁵*The light shines in the darkness, and the darkness can never extinguish it. ~John 1:5 NLT*

God helped me to understand that I would find the spirit of life within me, rather than on the outside, where darkness dwells. The Bible tells us that much of what lies outside ourselves is not of God but of the world.

> ¹⁶*"For all that is in the world, the lust of the flesh and the lust of the eyes and the boastful pride of life, is not from the Father, but is from the world." ~1 John 2:16 NASB*

Messiah lives within us, and we need to be led by God's indwelling Spirit, rather than that which is outside ourselves.

MY REVELATION OF THE TWO SPIRITS

After God allowed me to see into the spirit realm, I prayed for revelation of what I saw that night, and I am still praying for a complete understanding of all that I saw. The first revelation I received came while I was watching a movie on television. As a horrific event was about to unfold in this movie, ominous music began to play. When I heard the music, I realized it was literally a musical manifestation of the darkness. It was as if the darkness became music. Hollywood producers know exactly what type of music to play in their movies to instill fear and accentuate whatever evil event is about to unfold.

Through this revelation, I began to see more clearly how the spirit of darkness is able to project itself into the material world. Whether it be through music, books, television, the media, the words of family and friends, our dreams, or even our own thoughts, we need to be able to discern what is coming from the realm of darkness.

An insight I received concerning the Spirit of life came from a memory of when I was approximately nine years old. On that day, I was riding my bicycle up a hill, when I thought to myself, "Wouldn't it be great if this bicycle would go all by itself without having to pedal it, and I could just sit back and enjoy the ride?" As I remembered this, I thought to myself, "If the spirit of sealed, self-contained white life that I saw lived inside of me, I would have a life force in me that would be my engine, so I wouldn't have to push so hard, and I could just sit back and enjoy the ride."

The LORD revealed to me that His Spirit within me is my life force. It's taken me many years to come to this realization, and I'm still striving to live in this truth. I still have a long way to go, in order to fully live in this reality, but there has been a birthing that's taken place in my life, allowing God to be my life force.

Once you allow God's Spirit to be your life force, you will enter into a rest in Him. Instead of constantly struggling on your own, because you think it is all up to you, you will instead begin to trust God, knowing that He is going before you, working on your behalf, both in you and in your circumstances. Knowing that you don't have to control everything, that it doesn't all depend on you and that you can trust God, releases many burdens and produces rest. Yeshua spoke of this when He said:

> [28]*"Come to me, all you who are weary and burdened, and I will give you rest.* [29]*Take my yoke upon you and learn from me, for I am gentle and humble in heart, and you will find rest for your souls.* [30]*For my yoke is easy and my burden is light." ~Matthew 11:28-30 NIV*

You may be asking yourself, "If Yeshua's yoke is easy and His burden is light, why is my life so hard?" The reason is you're not letting Him be your life.

> [12]*"He who has the Son has life; he who does not have the Son of God does not have life." ~1 John 5:12 NIV*

Because of our reliance on trying to accomplish everything in our own flesh, we have a hard time receiving the revelation that our life is in the Son. We don't know how to lay down our own initiatives and allow God to arise and be God. We think we have to do it all ourselves, so we end up tired and burned out.

In order to strip us of our self-reliance and our reliance on others and the world, the LORD will often bring us into difficult circumstances we are unable to deal with on our own. In other words, He will place us in situations where only He can help us, in order to cause us to look to Him alone. An example of God doing this is found in Deuteronomy 8.

> [2]*"You shall remember all the way which the LORD your God has led you in the wilderness these forty years, that He might humble you, testing you, to know what was in your heart, whether you would keep His commandments or not. [3]He humbled you and let you be hungry, and fed you with manna which you did not know, nor did your fathers know, that He might make you understand that man does not live by bread alone, but man lives by everything that proceeds out of the mouth of the LORD. [4]Your clothing did not wear out on you, nor did your foot swell these forty years. [5]Thus you are to know in your heart that the LORD your God was disciplining you just as a man disciplines his son... [15]He led you through the great and terrible*

> *wilderness, with its fiery serpents and scorpions and thirsty ground where there was no water; He brought water for you out of the rock of flint.* ¹⁶*In the wilderness He fed you manna which your fathers did not know, that He might humble you and that He might test you, to do good for you in the end.* ¹⁷*Otherwise, you may say in your heart, 'My power and the strength of my hand made me this wealth.'"* ~Deuteronomy 8:2-5,15-17 NASB

This section of scripture shows us how the LORD was training Israel to look to Him *alone*. He severed them from relying on all other means and was teaching them that He *alone* was their source. In the New Testament, we find the LORD again dealing with the apostle Paul (Shaul) in like manner.

> ⁸*"For we do not want you to be unaware, brethren, of our affliction which came to us in Asia, that we were burdened excessively, beyond our strength, so that we despaired even of life;* ⁹*indeed, we had the sentence of death within ourselves so that we would not trust in ourselves, but in God who raises the dead;"* ~2 Corinthians 1:8-9 NASB

> ⁷*"Because of the surpassing greatness of the revelations, for this reason, to keep me from exalting myself, there was given me a thorn in the flesh, a messenger of Satan to torment me--to keep me from exalting myself!* ⁸*Concerning this I implored the Lord three times that it might leave me.* ⁹*And He has said to me, 'My grace is sufficient for you, for power is perfected in weakness.' Most gladly, therefore, I will rather boast about my weaknesses, so that the power of (Messiah) may dwell in me.* ¹⁰*Therefore I am well content with weaknesses, with insults, with distresses, with persecutions, with*

*difficulties, for (Messiah's) sake; for when I am weak,
then I am strong." ~2 Corinthians 12:7-10 NASB*

Once again, we can see by the LORD's dealings with Paul
(Shaul), that in order for us to live a life by the power of the
LORD's Spirit, Yahweh must first break us of self-reliance and
looking for our help from anything or anyone else but Him.

God desires for you to completely trust and look to Him
alone for all things. Once the LORD has stripped you of
relying on yourself and the world and has strengthened your
faith to believe that He is going before you, supplying all
your needs, you'll enter into greater rest and peace.

The LORD desires for you to have the same peace the
apostle John (Yochanan) experienced while celebrating
Passover with Yeshua. John simply leaned his head on Yeshua's
bosom and rested. You can experience this same peace for
your own life when you learn to trust in God and stop relying
on yourself, others, and the world to supply all your needs.

In conclusion, I believe the Spirit of life the LORD
showed me that night was the Ruach HaKodesh (Holy
Spirit) which He literally places within all His children. As
the LORD strips us of relying on ourselves and the world,
to trust in Him instead, we are then able to live by His life
that is within us.

ENCOUNTERING THE HOLY SPIRIT

We see in scripture that the Holy Spirit reveals Himself
in different ways. When Yeshua was baptized in the Jordan
River, the Spirit revealed Himself as a dove.

*[16]As soon as Jesus was baptized, he went up out of
the water. At that moment heaven was opened, and
he saw the Spirit of God descending like a dove and*

> *lighting on him.* ¹⁷*And a voice from heaven said, "This
> is my Son, whom I love; with him I am well pleased."*
> ~Matthew 3:16-17 NIV

On Pentecost (Shavuot), the Spirit revealed Himself as
a tongue of fire.

> ¹*When the day of Pentecost came, they were all together
> in one place.* ²*Suddenly a sound like the blowing of a
> violent wind came from heaven and filled the whole
> house where they were sitting.* ³*They saw what seemed
> to be tongues of fire that separated and came to rest on
> each of them.* ⁴*All of them were filled with the Holy
> Spirit and began to speak in other tongues as the Spirit
> enabled them.* ~Acts 2:1-4 NIV

In 1981, I started going through a season of what the
Bible calls repentance. The LORD began revealing certain
things in my life which I needed to turn away from, one
of them being cigarettes. One morning, while I was sitting
in a chair drinking a cup of tea, which had replaced the
cigarettes, the Holy Spirit suddenly appeared above my
head. It wasn't a thought or a mental picture in my mind;
the Spirit of God literally appeared above my head, twirling
around in all the colors of a rainbow.

Then, all of a sudden, He came through my head taking
possession of my inner man. He spoke these four simple
words, "I am a servant," in and through me. I heard His
voice as clearly as I can hear my own voice, but not through
my ears, although it was as solid and precise, as if it was
through my ears. Then as quickly as the encounter started,
it was over just like that.

This experience was not some vague feeling or mental
impression; rather, the power of God came upon me
suddenly. I could not have helped the experience along nor

could I have stopped it from happening. I've been praying since 1981 to better understand this experience and for revelation concerning those words He spoke to me, "I am a servant."

Ever since the day the Spirit of God appeared above my head in all the colors of the rainbow, I often wear rainbow-colored garments to remind me of that experience. For example, if you have watched my television broadcast, *Discovering the Jewish Jesus*, you may have seen me wearing a black or white robe with rainbow colors around the bottom and on the sleeves. I also wear these garments when I minister during God's appointed holiday, the Feast of Tabernacles (Sukkot).

Both the prophet Ezekiel (Yechezkiel) and the apostle John (Yochanan) had visions of Yahweh surrounded by a rainbow.

> [28] *Like the appearance of a rainbow in the clouds on a rainy day, so was the radiance around him. This was the appearance of the likeness of the glory of the LORD. When I saw it, I fell facedown, and I heard the voice of one speaking. -Ezekiel 1:28 NIV*

> [3] *And the one who sat there had the appearance of jasper and carnelian. A rainbow, resembling an emerald, encircled the throne. -Revelation 4:3 NIV*

This encounter with the Holy Spirit appearing above my head in all the colors of the rainbow, filling me and speaking through me, was so profound that I responded to it by joining a monastery to become a monk. But after three days of all the rituals, I realized that this wasn't where the LORD was leading me.

SEEKING A GREATER
AWARENESS OF THE HOLY SPIRIT

The encounters I have had with God, by His Spirit, have created within me a passion to seek the reality of His presence in my life. I don't want to wait until I die and go to heaven to experience His presence. I want to experience it right here and right now.

The reason I have shared my experiences with you is not to suggest that you need to have these types of experiences; rather, I'm sharing them with you so that you might know the scientific reality that the Holy Spirit is real, and He is within you. My desire is to help you gain a greater awareness that God's Spirit literally lives inside you.

After my encounter with the Holy Spirit, I was on fire for God. I started attending church, but so often it seemed like no matter what subject the sermon was on, they all ended the same way; my problems would be solved, and I would have what I wanted in life, if I just read the Bible more, prayed more, gave more money, and witnessed more.

As far as I knew, I was doing all these things as much as possible. I was reading my Bible every day, praying three hours a day, giving more than a tithe of my income, and if you were behind me in line at the grocery store, I'd turn around and witness to you. After ten years of doing all these things, however, God's presence still seemed to be far away. Although the LORD had supernaturally come to me several times in the experiences I've described to you, I was not experiencing intimacy with Him on a daily basis, and His lasting presence still seemed to be far away.

Then one day, I heard a teaching that said the secret to intimacy and experiencing God's presence was to pray the Lord's Prayer (Matthew 6:9-13). I said to myself with excitement, "That must be it! That's what I'm missing! I've been doing all these other things for so long, but praying the Lord's Prayer must be the answer!"

So I started praying the Lord's Prayer. First, I did it 15 minutes a day; nothing seemed to happen, so I increased it to 30 minutes. Still nothing happened, so I increased it to an hour a day. To me, if I wasn't talking, I wasn't praying. My mouth was going continuously for an hour a day; still nothing happened. I increased it to two hours a day; still nothing happened. In desperation, I increased it to three hours a day. I kid you not, I would sit and pray the Lord's Prayer for three hours a day. My mouth was going continuously for three hours; still nothing happened.

Then I thought, maybe I was talking too much, so I started praying an hour and a half and then listening for an hour and a half. Still nothing happened. Then I decided I would just sit and listen for three hours. I fell asleep. Nothing I did seemed to bring me into the intimacy with God I desired or into an awareness of His presence, until He finally helped me understand that I was searching for Him in all the wrong places.

For ten years, I had been searching for Him through all my works: reading the Bible, praying, giving money, and witnessing. The harder I worked at doing all those things, the more dissatisfied and burned out I became. Finally, when I got to a state of total burnout, God broke in and said, "Kirt, you're looking for Me on the outside. I'm inside you. I just want you to learn to sit before Me, be still, and let go of everything. I only want you to look to Me for one thing: the revelation that My Spirit is in you." I can tell you, as God is my witness, this is when everything started to change for me, and a new power infused my life!

43

YESHUA TAUGHT THAT HIS SPIRIT IS THE KEY

> [7]*"But I tell you the truth: It is for your good that I am going away. Unless I go away, the Counselor will not come to you; but if I go, I will send him to you." ~John 16:7 NIV*

Yeshua did not tell His disciples that "it was good that He was going away," in order to send them a New King James Bible; rather, He told them "it was good that He was going away," so He could send them the Counselor, the Ruach HaKodesh (Holy Spirit). Don't misunderstand me. I'm not telling you to give up Bible reading. We need to read the scriptures to show ourselves to be an approved workman of the LORD.

> [15]*Do your best to present yourself to God as one approved, a workman who does not need to be ashamed and who correctly handles the word of truth. ~2 Timothy 2:15 NIV*

Knowing God's Word is a lot like being a carpenter. A carpenter has many tools, and the more tools he has, the more jobs he's able to perform. The more of God's Word that you know, the more you will be able to utilize it, just as a carpenter utilizes a specific tool for the project he's doing.

You'll never hear me preach a word that's not right out of the Word of God, but today we've made the Bible our main focus instead of God. The scriptures are designed to lead us to God, not replace Him. If you think about it, those first disciples didn't even have Bibles like we know them today. It was the Spirit of God who led them in all truth.

> [13]*"But when he, the Spirit of truth, comes, he will guide you into all truth. He will not speak on his own; he will speak only what he hears, and he will tell you what is yet to come." ~John 16:13 NIV*

The Spirit was their sufficiency. The written Word (the Bible) was never designed to replace the Living Word (Yeshua). Yet, I believe the church today, for the most part, has placed almost all emphasis on God's written Word and not enough on His Living Word (Yeshua).

Yeshua spoke to the Pharisees about their diligent study of the scriptures.

> [39]*"You diligently study the Scriptures because you think that by them you possess eternal life. These are the Scriptures that testify about me, [40]yet you refuse to come to me to have life." ~John 5:39-40 NIV*

The Pharisees knew the scriptures extremely well. They studied them night and day, yet they still rejected Yeshua. You can know the Bible very well and still be completely deceived just like the Pharisees, unless you have the Spirit, the One who wrote the Bible, to give you revelation.

It is the Spirit, alone, who reveals the things of God. Even if you memorize the Bible, unless you're depending on the Spirit to give you revelation, it won't profit you. It could actually do you more harm than good, making you judgmental of others, or making you feel condemned, if you aren't meeting its standard.

Don't misunderstand what I am saying. I love God's written Word. I memorize it, chew it, and digest it. It is the Word of Yeshua and the Word of Yahweh. It cleanses, transforms, gives direction, and brings us into the truth. There must be, however, a marriage between God's written

Word (the Bible) and His Living Word (Yeshua) by the Holy
Spirit in our lives.

Only the Spirit knows the thoughts of God, and He's
been given to us so that we may know the things of God.

> [12]*We have not received the spirit of the world but the
> Spirit who is from God, that we may understand what
> God has freely given us.* ~1 Corinthians 2:12 NIV

We are unable to perceive the things of God by the
natural realm, our eyes, ears, and minds, but God gives us
revelation through His Spirit.

God desires for us to understand that the Spirit is real,
and that He lives inside us. We need to stop searching for
Him outside ourselves. Have you been searching for God in
the things you are doing and in the places you are running
to? Are you forever reading books in order to find God?
Books are helpful, but the reality is that God has placed His
Spirit within us, and it's through His Spirit that we will find
Him. The scripture says in the book of Romans:

> [11]*But if the Spirit of Him who raised Jesus from the
> dead dwells in you, He who raised (Messiah) Jesus
> from the dead will also give life to your mortal bodies
> through His Spirit who dwells in you...* [13]*for if you
> are living according to the flesh, you must die; but if
> by the Spirit you are putting to death the deeds of the
> body, you will live.* [14]*For all who are being led by the
> Spirit of God, these are sons of God.* [15]*For you have
> not received a spirit of slavery leading to fear again,
> but you have received a spirit of adoption as sons by
> which we cry out, "Abba! Father!"* [16]*The Spirit Himself
> testifies with our spirit that we are children of God.*
> ~Romans 8:11, 13-16 NASB

ABIDING IN THE SPIRI

As we learn to abide in Messiah, tru
within us, we will enter into a place of
psalmist knew the importance of this.

> [1] *He who dwells in the shelter of the Most High will rest
> in the shadow of the Almighty. -Psalm 91:1 NIV*

When we attempt to live our lives on our own,
failing to trust and abide in the Spirit, we will end up
stumbling through life without His help and protection.
Somehow, we seem to believe that if we don't do something
ourselves, it won't get done. Actually, the opposite is true.
When we abide in the Spirit and depend on Him, more
is accomplished through His power, than could ever
have been accomplished on our own. This is why, in 2
Corinthians 12, Paul (Shaul) boasted in his weaknesses,
because when he depended on the LORD in his weakness,
the power of God was strong in and through his life.
This dependency is a daily process that God is continually
circumcising our hearts with.

In 2006, I went to the Kansas City International House
of Prayer (IHOP) where there has been 24-hour prayer going
on night and day, seven days a week since September 1999.
I went there at a crisis time in my life when I was really
hurting inside. The LORD was leading me to simply sit at
His feet and wait upon Him.

The story of Mary (Miryam) and Martha (Marta)
demonstrates the importance of just sitting and waiting
upon the Lord. It contrasts two sisters: Martha who was
busy doing so many things for Yeshua and Mary who simply
sat at His feet to receive from Him. Martha became upset
at Mary, because she wasn't helping her with all the meal
preparations. Martha asked Yeshua to tell her sister to help

.. Instead, Yeshua told Martha that her sister, Mary, who
ad chosen to simply sit at His feet and receive, had chosen
what is better.

> [38]*As Jesus and his disciples were on their way, he came
> to a village where a woman named Martha opened
> her home to him.* [39]*She had a sister called Mary, who
> sat at the Lord's feet listening to what he said.* [40]*But
> Martha was distracted by all the preparations that
> had to be made. She came to him and asked, "Lord,
> don't you care that my sister has left me to do the work
> by myself? Tell her to help me!"* [41]*"Martha, Martha,"
> the Lord answered, "you are worried and upset about
> many things,* [42]*but only one thing is needed. Mary has
> chosen what is better, and it will not be taken away
> from her."* ~Luke 10:38-42 NIV*

What higher act of service could Martha have been
given than to prepare a meal for Yeshua? Yet, Yeshua said
that Mary had chosen to do the most important thing,
which is just to simply sit at the Lord's feet and receive from
Him. So I want to encourage you to be more like Mary.

The truth is God wants to make known to us that we
don't need to be better *doers*; we need to be better *receivers*.
Our lives should be that of continuously receiving from
the LORD so that our doing will just be an overflow of
our receiving. As we make our priority receiving, rather
than doing, we will bear much fruit, fruit that can only be
produced when we abide in Him.

> [5]*"I am the vine, you are the branches; he who abides in
> Me and I in him, he bears much fruit, for apart from
> Me you can do nothing."* ~John 15:5 NASB

Yeshua spoke of the importance of abiding in the Father. He did nothing of His own initiative; it was the Father abiding in Him who did all the works.

> [10]*"Do you not believe that I am in the Father, and the Father is in Me? The words that I say to you I do not speak on My own initiative, but the Father abiding in Me does His works." -John 14:10 NASB*

It should be the same with us. We should do nothing of our own initiative; instead, allow Yeshua, through the Spirit within us, to do all the works. The goal is to abide in Yeshua, even as Yeshua abides in us.

EXPERIENCING THE PEACE OF GOD

When I returned from IHOP, the LORD led me to start a 24-hour prayer room that we call the Key of David in our Messianic synagogue, Adat Adonai (www.adatadonai.com). By the favor and grace of God, there has been someone in our prayer room continuously, 24 hours a day, 365 days a year since February 14, 2007, when we offered up the Key of David to Yeshua as a love gift and living memorial to Him on Valentine's Day.

This is truly a miracle of God, since we only have approximately 120 members in our congregation (as of 2010). There have been several congregations consisting of over a thousand members who have failed in their attempt to keep a 24-hour prayer room going, because they didn't have enough volunteers in their congregation to maintain it. Our goal is to have someone in our prayer room, 24 hours a day, 7 days a week, until Yeshua's return. The fact that we've been able to maintain this 24/7 prayer room commitment since February 2007 is the result of the blessing of God, and we give Him alone the glory and credit for it.

When we opened our prayer room, I stopped doing many of the things I had been doing, so I could just sit and wait upon God. I delegated many of my ministry responsibilities to others, and I stopped actively scheduling appointments to travel and minister at churches. My wife, Cynthia, also had the same call upon her life. She gave up a high-paying job in order to sit and wait upon God.

My wife and I were now placed in a position of totally relying and trusting upon God for our provision, since our only income would be a small amount from the synagogue. God was placing us in a position where He could now arise in our lives and prove Himself.

I was committed to stopping all my activities in order to let God completely take over. I had reached a place where I was tired of wondering whether it was me who was making things happen or whether it was Him. The only way I could know that it was Him was for me to stop, so I could see Him do it; and, beloved, He did. He gave me more peace, strengthened my marriage, and opened up a worldwide ministry. Praise Yahweh! Thank you LORD!

As I began to sit and wait upon the LORD in the prayer room, a new peace (shalom) began to emerge in my life. It was real! Everyone in the congregation saw it. My wife and children saw it. My neighbors saw it. By simply sitting in the prayer room and waiting on God, I received an infusion of Yeshua, and what's more, God blessed my circumstances.

> [33]*"But seek first His kingdom and His righteousness, and all these things will be added to you." -Matthew 6:33 NASB*

In our prayer room beautiful worship music is played continuously. The worship music played is called vertical worship music. It is songs of music sung to God rather than songs about Him. When you actually sing to God, intimacy and relationship is developed.

A careful study of the scriptures reveals that the LORD often communicates through the agency of music. Music tenderizes the heart and opens us up to receive from Him. When the prophet Elijah (Eliyahu) called for the minstrel, the Spirit of God came upon him.

> [15]*"But now bring me a minstrel." And it came about, when the minstrel played, that the hand of the LORD came upon him. ~2 Kings 3:15 NASB*

When King Saul was tormented by an evil spirit, David would come and play his harp. When David played, the evil spirit would leave.

> [23]*So it came about whenever the evil spirit from God came to Saul, David would take the harp and play it with his hand; and Saul would be refreshed and be well, and the evil spirit would depart from him. ~1 Samuel 16:23 NASB*

Yeshua connected the gift of the Holy Spirit with shalom (peace).

> [26]*"But the Counselor, the Holy Spirit, whom the Father will send in my name, will teach you all things and will remind you of everything I have said to you.* [27]*Peace I leave with you; my peace I give you. I do not give to you as the world gives. Do not let your hearts be troubled and do not be afraid." ~John 14:26-27 NIV*

Permanent peace will never be found on the outside. Peace that is rooted in circumstances will never last, because our circumstances are constantly changing, but the peace that Yeshua can give us is solid and enduring. His Spirit is peace, and that is why Yeshua is called the Prince of Peace (Sar Shalom). Just as Yeshua calmed the sea for His disciples, He can calm any storm that comes in your life and bring you peace.

> [26] *He replied, "You of little faith, why are you so afraid?" Then he got up and rebuked the winds and the waves, and it was completely calm. ~Matthew 8:26 NIV*

The same Spirit of peace that calmed the storm is inside us. I spent many years, as a believer, searching for God on the outside, not realizing He was already in me. When we grasp a hold of this reality, we will have greater peace in our lives.

Yeshua desires to breathe His peace into us, even as He breathed the peace of His Holy Spirit into His disciples.

> [21] *So Jesus said to them again, "Peace be with you;" ...* [22] *And when He had said this, He breathed on them and said to them, "Receive the Holy Spirit." ~John 20:21a, 22 NASB*

When you receive the Holy Spirit, as a believer in Yeshua, you receive that same impartation of peace that Yeshua breathed on His disciples. The more that you enter into this peace, the greater ability you will have to discern the heart and mind of God's Spirit.

The book of Revelation gives us a picture of this unshakable peace that Yahweh infuses our hearts with.

> [6] *Also before the throne there was what looked like a sea of glass, clear as crystal. ~Revelation 4:6a NIV*

The sea of glass before the throne of God speaks of an absolute stillness where there is no worry, anxiety, or fear.

When you think about it, a sheet of glass has no ripples in it. This speaks of the fact that there is no disturbance in God. His heart and mind is perfectly calm, even as a flat sea is a calm sea. This sea of glass in heaven is a picture of the perfect peace God is bringing us into, as we draw near to Him.

To truly experience God's peace, we must come out of the world and spend time sitting in His presence. When we do, He will give us greater revelation and strengthen our inner man by His Spirit. Paul (Shaul) prayed:

> [17] *that the God of our Lord Jesus (Messiah), the Father of glory, may give to you a spirit of wisdom and of revelation in the knowledge of Him.* [18] *I pray that the eyes of your heart may be enlightened, so that you will know what is the hope of His calling, what are the riches of the glory of His inheritance in the saints,* [19] *and what is the surpassing greatness of His power toward us who believe. These are in accordance with the working of the strength of His might* [20] *which He brought about in (Messiah), when He raised Him from the dead and seated Him at His right hand in the heavenly places,...* [14] *For this reason I bow my knees before the Father,...* [16] *that He would grant you, according to the riches of His glory, to be strengthened with power through His Spirit in the inner man,* ~Ephesians 1:17-20; 3:14,16 NASB*

As you are strengthened in His peace, you will also be able to break off the bondage of Satan's power from your life.

> [20] *The God of peace will soon crush Satan under your feet.* ~Romans 16:20a NIV*

A DWELLING PLACE FOR GOD

David desired to build a Temple in which Yahweh could dwell among Israel.

> [3]*"I will not enter my house or go to my bed-* [4]*I will allow no sleep to my eyes, no slumber to my eyelids,* [5]*till I find a place for the LORD, a dwelling for the Mighty One of Jacob." -Psalm 132:3-5 NIV*

Our goal, too, should be to build a dwelling place for God. Yahweh no longer dwells in physical structures, such as the Temple, but now dwells within us, the body of Messiah.

> [16]*Don't you know that you yourselves are God's temple and that God's Spirit lives in you? -1 Corinthians 3:16 NIV*

We have literally become the dwelling place of the LORD, and when we spend time sitting before Him, He will transform our hearts and thoughts to become like His. The more we discipline ourselves to sit before Him to transform us, the more He will align us with Himself and conform us to the image of His Son. As we are transformed and conformed to the image of His Son, we will be brought into greater peace. Even as the LORD incarnated Himself in Messiah, Jesus, so He wants to incarnate Himself in us and through us. When we arrive at this state, oh, what blessed peace there will be, beloved.

WAITING UPON THE LORD

Three months after opening our prayer room, I received a phone call from the pastor who owned the building we were using for our synagogue. He informed me that the building had been sold, and we needed to be out in 30 days.

After I received this phone call, I said to the LORD, "I have waited on You for inner transformation, and as a result, I have more peace and power and authority in my life than ever before. It's tangible and real! People see it, and I feel it. Just as I've waited on You for inner transformation and You anchored me and changed me on the inside, now I'm going to wait on You to see You act in my outer circumstances."

What I am saying, beloved, is that I had experienced God's workings within me, and now I would be trusting Him with the outer circumstances of my life. I made a decision to fully trust Him with the need our congregation now had for a building.

In the natural, I would have been running around like a chicken with its head cut off, hustling to find another building; instead, I chose to trust and wait upon God. By handling this situation in this manner, I was giving God an opportunity to prove Himself. The day I received the phone call, informing me that our congregation needed to be out of the building in 30 days, I didn't even let anyone from the congregation know the building was sold.

I felt the LORD leading me to just wait upon Him for a period of two weeks, until May 14, before doing anything. This meant that the congregation would only have two weeks left to be out of the building, after I had waited upon God until May 14. It was a blind test of faith; we had no place to go. Adat Adonai (Hebrew for the "Congregation of the LORD") had never owned their own building in the 18 years of their existence because of financial limitations, but I was believing God that we would be in our own building by Rosh HaShana, the Jewish New Year, (which was in approximately four months), even though we still didn't have the necessary funds.

On Shabbat, three days after I had been informed that the building had been sold, I informed the congregation of our predicament. I also told them the LORD had instructed me to do absolutely nothing but wait upon Him for two weeks and assured them that Adat Adonai would own its first building by Rosh HaShana.

Following the worship service, people came up to me and asked, "Rabbi, what are you going to do?" I told them, "I'm just going to wait on the LORD. He has instructed me to wait on Him for two weeks." They said, "Great, but what are you going to do?" I told them again, "I'm just going to wait on the LORD." They said, "Great, but what are you going to do?" They didn't get it! I wasn't going to do anything but wait upon the LORD. I believed that God would either bring us a building, as I waited on Him, or He would bless me after the two weeks of waiting with the right building.

The LORD did not bring us a building during the two week period of waiting on Him, but I felt confident that He would direct me to the right building, now that I had waited on Him, putting Him first. With my two weeks of waiting now up, I felt released to get busy, putting my business skills and Jewish ingenuity to use in finding the right building. I felt like Joshua taking possession of the Promised Land, believing God's blessing was on me, giving me success.

With just 14 days left to be out of the building, I started making phone calls to realtors, but not one of them returned my call that day. For the first time, my faith began to shrink. I thought to myself, "Have I been totally irresponsible? How many pastors in this city would have left their congregation in this type of a predicament of having to be out of a building in less than two weeks with no idea of where to go? What type of irresponsible leader are you? You should have been planning for this situation two years ago." All these accusations came upon me. Had I been irresponsible? Had I exercised poor leadership?

That night I had a dream, and in the dream, I saw myself crying out to God in excruciating pain. I could literally feel the pain of my soul, as I cried out to God saying, "I trusted You in this. I told Your people that You supernaturally led us into this building, and that You would supernaturally lead us to the next place, when it was time. I obeyed You and waited upon You. Now here I am with no place to go."

I felt abandoned and forsaken in the dream, and it was very, very painful. Then all of a sudden in the dream, as I was crying to God, a golden spear appeared, approximately two feet long by one inch wide. This golden spear pierced right through my forehead and out through the back of my neck. Then the Spirit of God said, "You've obeyed me to the end in this. You didn't panic, and you trusted Me. You didn't take matters into your own hands or act in your own initiative. You waited on Me. Now I've slain you with My truth, and Kirt, it is now your possession. You will be able to live the rest of your life waiting upon Me, seeing Me go before you doing the work."

When I awoke from the dream, I felt encouraged, but I still had no idea where our congregation would go. That morning I started calling some pastors in the area to see if they would allow us to temporarily meet in their building. I quickly was able to find a pastor who invited us to share his congregation's building until we found our own place. At least for now, we had someplace to go.

RECEIVING A PROPHETIC WORD

A few days later, I received a call from a member of our congregation who told me that she had received a prophetic word for me while she was in our prayer room. This individual had been a member of our congregation for four years. She was very soft-spoken and had never brought me a prophetic word before. She told me, "The LORD says, 'I gave you May 14th, and now I give you June 14th. On June 14th you will have your building.'" You may remember that May 14th was the last day of the two week period of waiting on the LORD. When she called me with this prophetic word, I was very encouraged, but I also thought, "Okay we'll see."

Over the years, I had many people give me what they claimed to be a prophetic word from God. My experience has been that many people who claim to have a prophetic word are well-intentioned, but oftentimes are not actually delivering a true word from God. I have had a few instances where I did receive, from an individual, a truly prophetic word from God that did in fact come to pass. Most of the time, however, that which was claimed to be a prophetic word from God was not. So in this case, I was encouraged but had a wait to see attitude.

THE NEW BUILDING

As I was searching for God's direction, a realtor took me to see an old VFW hall in the inner city of Toledo. It was the only available property that was both large enough and in the price range that we could afford, since we only had approximately $35,000 in the bank. If we decided to purchase this building, our Messianic congregation would be moving from the suburbs to the inner city. Personally, I was thrilled! I had always had a heart for the African-American community, and this property was located in a multicultural setting.

I presented an offer to the realtor, who in turn presented it to the trustees of the VFW hall. The trustees decided they would present the offer to the general membership for a vote, "a week from Thursday."

The day I was informed that the VFW trustees would be presenting our offer to the general membership for a vote, I was having dinner with a member from the congregation. While we were eating, I told him the offer would be presented to the general membership a week from Thursday, and as he looked at his Pocket Palm, he said, "That's June 14th!" I hadn't realized that date was June 14th. I lifted my hand up and said, "If they accept our offer on June 14th, that's our building." Then I gave him a high five. The realtor had absolutely no idea that I had received a prophetic word for June 14th.

Late in the day on June 14th, I received a call from the realtor congratulating me that our offer was accepted. I was ecstatic! I came before the congregation with the blowing of shofars, declaring that God had arisen and proved Himself. It was incredible! The entire congregation, except for a few, was behind the purchase, and we were excited!

The realtor believed the only changes that would be necessary to bring the building up to code would be making the bathrooms handicap accessible. I hired an architect to inspect the building to insure that no other changes would be necessary and to draw up a plan to present to the city's building committee to bring the bathrooms up to code. I was filled with hope and excitement about reaching the inner city of Toledo for Messiah!

As I was driving to the synagogue one day, contemplating all of this, I was having one of my best experiences with God that I have ever had. I was on top of the world, flying in my trust in the LORD! I was thinking how incredible it was, of how I had waited on God to bring us the right building, and how He had arisen and proved Himself. I told Him, "You're so faithful! I trust You! You love me so much, and

Your favor is on me! This is so incredible! Nothing is going to stop me now!"

Immediately after saying this, my phone rang; it was the architect telling me there would be many other things in the building that would need to be brought up to code. The estimated cost was $150,000 to $200,000. I was immediately jolted from the spiritual high I had been emotionally experiencing. This additional cost wasn't to remodel the building; it was only to bring the building up to code. Furthermore, this additional cost was more than we were actually paying for the building, which was $168,000. The cost to purchase the building and bring it up to code was now $368,000; our congregation didn't have that kind of money!

It felt as though I had been kicked into orbit and didn't know how to get my feet back on the ground. I cried out to the LORD saying, "What's going on? Did You set me up, just to humiliate me and expose me as a false prophet? My ministry is over! No one will ever have confidence in me again."

As I continued driving to the synagogue, I calmed down and thought, "LORD, there must be one of three things going on: either You set me up to humiliate me, because You don't want me to lead this congregation anymore, or somehow You're going to have the code requirements waived, or You'll miraculously provide us the $200,000 to bring the building up to code."

When I reached the synagogue, I got down on my knees in the prayer room and prayed all day. I thought to myself, "LORD, maybe You had us go into contract on the VFW building, knowing it wouldn't go through, in order to take us out of the market until the property You have for us becomes available on the market."

The next day when I got to the synagogue, there was a lady standing in the parking lot I had never seen before. As

I approached her, she asked me if there was someone here in authority from Adat Adonai, because she had seen a sign in front of the church which said, "Temporary Home of Adat Adonai." I told her I was the rabbi, and she explained that she was a realtor and had just received a listing on a building our congregation might be interested in purchasing.

I went with her to see the building. It was on several acres of land in a beautiful suburban neighborhood in Ottawa Lake, Michigan, just outside Toledo, close to the Jewish population. Well, to make a long story short, we ended up purchasing the building, and we closed on the building the same exact day we were scheduled to close on the VFW building. I truly believe the LORD purposely kept us busy in the process of purchasing the VFW building until the building God desired for us became available on the market.

The amazing thing about the purchase of this building was that we never could have put together the specific deal we needed with the sellers, unless we had worked with this specific realtor. She was a good friend of the people selling the building, and through a mutual Christian relationship, we were able to put together a deal in which we could afford to purchase the building.

The building God blessed our synagogue with was absolutely incredible! I know if I had taken matters into my own hands, we never would have received such an incredible blessing from the LORD. It all happened, because I stopped my self-initiative. I waited and trusted the LORD to do the work, and in the end, He proved Himself.

The LORD desires to prove Himself in your life. As you begin to stop your self-initiative and start waiting upon and trusting God to do the work, He will accomplish incredible things in your own life. You will be able to achieve these things, as you gain a greater awareness of God's Spirit living within you.

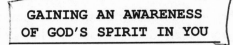

GAINING AN AWARENESS OF GOD'S SPIRIT IN YOU

There are several action steps you can take in your life which will lead you into a greater awareness of God's Spirit dwelling within you.

1. SEPARATING YOURSELF FROM THE WORLD

The first of these steps involves turning away from the things of the world, to be separate unto Him.

> [17] *"Therefore come out from them and be separate, says the LORD. Touch no unclean thing, and I will receive you.* [18] *I will be a Father to you, and you will be my sons and daughters, says the LORD Almighty." -2 Corinthians 6:17-18 NIV*

In our culture, Satan attempts to draw us outside of ourselves in search of life. God has placed His Spirit within us, while the world outside ourselves lies in darkness. When we pursue the things of the world, we don't recognize that we are being led into darkness.

> [15] *Do not love the world nor the things in the world. If anyone loves the world, the love of the Father is not in him.* [16] *For all that is in the world, the lust of the flesh and the lust of the eyes and the boastful pride of life, is not from the Father, but is from the world. -1 John 2:15-16 NASB*

Friendship with the world means putting yourself in a f hostility towards God.

⁴*don't you know that friendship with the world is hatred toward God? Anyone who chooses to be a friend of the world becomes an enemy of God. ~James 4:4b NIV*

If you desire to live each day in the powerful revelation that Messiah is living in you, you must stop entangling yourself in the corrupt things of this world. You must stop watching on television, the very things that killed Yeshua. Stop listening to music that is mixed with lyrics of violence, sexuality, and self-ambition. Quit your constant busyness of running here and running there. When you have a problem, instead of discussing it with everyone you know, go immediately to the LORD and seek His wisdom and guidance. In doing so, you'll receive a greater awareness of His presence, and He will bring you into a much deeper experience with Himself.

2. ALLOWING GOD TO CLEANSE AND HEAL YOU

Another step that you can take which will lead you into a greater awareness of God's Spirit dwelling within you is to allow God to cleanse and heal you. God desires to cleanse and heal you of all your insecurities, anxieties, and fear that have been caused by sin. Instead of trying to cover up your insecurities, anxieties, fear, and sin with all the things of the world, allow Him to cleanse and heal you with Yeshua's blood and His Spirit.

When Adam and Eve sinned in the Garden of Eden, they suddenly became aware that they were naked. They immediately felt ashamed, embarrassed, and fearful. In their fear, they ran to cover their nakedness with the things of the world. For them, it was fig leaves. You probably aren't using fig leaves to cover up your insecurities, but are you using some addiction in your life that's drawing you deeper into darkness and pushing you further from God? Is the addiction you're using success, material things, illicit affairs, food, drugs, alcohol, codependent relationships, shopping, busyness, or excessive work?

Adam and Eve learned they couldn't run from their insecurities, and it wasn't until they finally turned to God that He was able to clothe their nakedness with animal skins. God is greater than any insecurity you may have! Stop running to the things of the world; instead, come to Him. He is the only One who can bring cleansing and healing to your life.

When Yeshua opened the scroll in the synagogue, He proclaimed that Yahweh had sent Him to heal the brokenhearted.

> [1]*The Spirit of the Sovereign LORD is on me, because the LORD has anointed me to preach good news to the poor. He has sent me to bind up the brokenhearted, to proclaim freedom for the captives and release from darkness for the prisoners,* -Isaiah 61:1 NIV

Now is the time to come to Yeshua, allowing Him, through the Holy Spirit (Ruach HaKodesh), to totally cleanse and heal you from the inside out.

3. STOP BLAMING OTHERS

Oftentimes, Satan deceives us into blaming others for our frustrations, unhappiness, and failures. This deception of blaming others leads to demonic anger towards others and traps us in darkness. As long as we blame others for our problems, we are ineffective in solving and overcoming them. It's only when we stop blaming others and accept responsibility for our own lives that God can cleanse us, heal us, and bring us into a deeper state of abiding in Him.

There was a time in my life when I was trapped in this deception of blaming others for my own frustrations; as a result, I was a very angry person. My wife, Cynthia, and I have very different personality types. She is very relational and easy going, and I tend to be very intense and driven. This mix became a challenge for me, when it came to being prompt for appointments. I like to be early, and Cynthia struggles with being on time. This was a continuous source of frustration for me.

We had been married for 15 years, and nothing I did seemed to change the situation. I tried asking, begging, pleading, and most of all screaming, but nothing I did or said changed her. One evening this conflict reached its climax. I had been gently bringing it up to Cynthia, throughout the week, that we had a very important appointment later that week, and we really needed to be on time.

When the evening came for us to leave our home for the appointment, I told Cynthia that I would be waiting for her in the car. I waited and waited and waited, and after approximately 15 minutes of waiting, I became so enraged that I literally almost rammed my car right through my garage. After coming so close to doing something so destructive, I recognized that my rage was completely out of control and that something was wrong with me. It really shook me up! After all, who would I have hurt by ramming my car through my own garage, but myself? I recognized that the issue was not simply a matter of me being frustrated because of my wife's lack of promptness, but that something was wrong with me.

I sat before the LORD for understanding in this, and as I did, He showed me that I had been blaming my wife for my own anger, rather than taking responsibility for it myself.

The problem was not just that my wife struggled with being late; rather, the problem was that I was not controlling my response to it. While waiting on God and being still before Him, I learned that I need to take responsibility for myself, rather than blaming others. This revelation brought great transformation in my life and furthered the sanctifying work of the Ruach HaKodesh within me.

4. DISCIPLINING YOURSELF TO BE STILL BEFORE GOD

You will gain a greater awareness of God's Spirit within you when you develop the spiritual discipline of being still before the LORD. The apostle Paul (Shaul) speaks of the importance of spiritual discipline. He tells us that physical discipline has some profit, but spiritual discipline is not only profitable now, but is profitable for an eternity.

> [8]*for bodily discipline is only of little profit, but godliness is profitable for all things, since it holds promise for the present life and also for the life to come. -1 Timothy 4:8 NASB*

We hear so little about spiritual discipline in our western church culture. Instead, we often try to make things as easy and convenient as possible for our congregants. Too often, we hear only what we want to hear, and there is little demand placed upon our lives. In fact, many have turned Yeshua into a magic genie who exists to grant our requests and have turned the message of the Gospel into a plan to achieve the American dream. I say all this to point out that self-discipline is, oftentimes, not included in the message that many of us are hearing today. The call to follow Yeshua is about the sacrifice of our own ambitions, and it involves self-discipline. Yeshua told us:

> [25]*"For whoever wishes to save his life will lose it; but whoever loses his life for My sake will find it."* ~Matthew 16:25 NASB

Yeshua also taught us:

> [38]*"and anyone who does not take his cross and follow me is not worthy of me."* ~Matthew 10:38 NIV

Before Yeshua went to the cross to be crucified, He prayed to the Father in the Garden of Gethsemane saying:

> [42]*"Father, if you are willing, take this cup from me; yet not my will, but yours be done."* ~Luke 22:42 NIV

Simply stated, beloved, if you are going to enter in through the straight and narrow way which leads to life, you must practice self-discipline in your life.

> [13]*"Enter through the narrow gate; for the gate is wide and the way is broad that leads to destruction, and there are many who enter through it.* [14]*For the gate is small and the way is narrow that leads to life, and there are few who find it."* ~Matthew 7:13-14 NASB

This self-discipline involves the practice of stilling yourself before God. The Psalmist knew the importance of being still before God.

> [10]*"Be still, and know that I am God;"* ~Psalm 46:10a NIV

What was true for the psalmist is true for all of us. As you learn to sit still before God and allow Him to minister to you, He will transform your life. He is the only One who can bring change. Even though you may feel nothing is happening as you sit before Him, trust the process. You probably won't see change in a single day, but over time, you will notice change in your life.

I recently had a dream in which I found myself sitting in a dark room across from a man, who I knew had been with me for a long time. He was at one side of the table, and I was on the other side. Somehow in the dream, I knew that this man was a familiar friend. I was tired of sitting across from this man, and I wanted to leave the room, because nothing seemed to be happening. It seemed boring! The LORD revealed to me that this man, whom I was sitting across from in this dark room in which nothing seemed to be happening, was Yeshua. The revelation that the LORD was communicating to me was that if I just keep spending time sitting across from Yeshua, He would make me whole.

As you sit before the LORD, He will bring you into a greater understanding of who you are in Him. This greater revelation of self-understanding will bring both a positive affirmation of your identity in Him as well as an understanding of the areas in your life where you have been deceived and need to repent.

As you spend time sitting in the LORD's presence and seeking Him, He promises that you, too, will be rewarded with transformation.

> [6]*And without faith it is impossible to please God, because anyone who comes to him must believe that he exists and that he rewards those who earnestly seek him. ~Hebrews 11:6 NIV*

I want to encourage you to get a room somewhere in your home and spend at least 30 minutes every day sitting before the LORD with beautiful vertical worship music playing. Vertical worship music CDs can be ordered through the Kansas City International House of Prayer web site at www.ihop.org. I strongly suggest that you watch their live stream vertical worship music which flows out of their 24/7 prayer room.

As you spend time sitting before the LORD, He will use the music as an agency of the Holy Spirit to impart Himself into your life. Start sitting before Him every day for 30 minutes. Everyone is capable of spending 30 minutes with God each day.

As time goes on, keep increasing the 30 minutes to an hour or more. It is of utter importance that you maintain your discipline in this every day, because once you allow an exception to come in, all your discipline will go right out the window. Even if you have to stay up late at night, because you were so busy that day, take the time to sit before the LORD seeking Him.

Adopt an attitude of receiving instead of striving. Allow the LORD to impart to you the revelation that His Spirit is within you. As you take time to come out of the world and spend time in stillness before Him, He will impart His peace to you through His Spirit. Even if you can't sense God's presence and feel as though nothing is happening, don't give up. God sees you and your desire to draw close to Him, and He will reward you as you continue to patiently sit before Him. Remember, this is not a sprint but a marathon.

CULTIVATING INTIMACY WITH GOD

The LORD speaks so many times in scripture about His unconditional love for us. He chose us out of the world before we were even born. We were not chosen because of anything we did, either good or bad, but simply because He chose to love us.

> [8]*But God demonstrates His own love toward us, in that while we were yet sinners, (Messiah) died for us.*
> *~Romans 5:8 NASB*

His love for us is like the love of a mother and father for their infant child. In Exodus 34:5-7, the LORD describes who He is to us. The first word God uses in describing who He is to us is the Hebrew word *rachum*. This word *rachum* comes from the Hebrew word meaning womb, and it communicates and reveals to us that the LORD loves us with the type of affection that a mother has for her infant child that comes from her womb. The LORD's love never changes, and He will never love you any more or any less than He already does right now.

God's greatest desire is to have intimacy with you. The desire of the LORD to have fellowship with His people is the constant theme of scripture. Even the Tabernacle, which the LORD commanded the children of Israel to build, was for the purpose of having intimacy with them.

> [8]*"Let them construct a sanctuary for Me, that I may dwell among them." ~Exodus 25:8 NASB*

Just as God desired to dwell among Israel, He desires to dwell among you. The LORD longs to have an intimacy with you that will bind you in oneness with Him. Several ways in which you can cultivate this intimacy with Him are through obedience, fasting, and spending time sitting still in His presence.

1. CULTIVATING INTIMACY THROUGH OBEDIENCE

> [21]"*Whoever has my commands and obeys them, he is the one who loves me. He who loves me will be loved by my Father, and I too will love him and show myself to him.*"... [23]*Jesus replied, "If anyone loves me, he will obey my teaching. My Father will love him, and we will come to him and make our home with him.*"
> ~John 14:21, 23 NIV

For many years this scripture verse troubled me. When I read it, it seemed to be saying that God would love me, if I obeyed Him. My understanding of God's love for me, being based on my obedience, deeply disturbed me and seemed to contradict so many other verses in scripture, which teach that God's love for us is unconditional.

As the years went by, Yeshua helped me to understand that what He was actually saying in this verse was that, as I give myself to Him, He will reveal His love to me. God's love for us never changes, but as we choose to love Him, He then reveals His love to us. In other words, He responds to us as we respond to Him. The reason we obey Him, is not to earn His love, rather we obey Him out of a desire to walk in oneness with Him.

In Deuteronomy 8, the LORD told the children of Israel that He loved them, even as a father loves his son, but He couldn't bring them into the Promised Land, until their hearts and character were prepared. John 14:21, 23 teaches this same thing. God loves us and desires to reveal Himself to us and make His home with us, but He will not do so, until we choose to love Him.

When Yeshua speaks of obedience, He isn't seeking obedience for obedience's sake, but rather obedience for the sake of love. Obedience produces a separation in your life unto God. As you come into more of a oneness with Yeshua, you will no longer be striving against Him. It won't be your way versus His way, but rather a joining together with Him. As you learn how to say, "LORD, not my will, but Thy will be done," you will enter into deeper and deeper intimacy with God.

2. CULTIVATING INTIMACY THROUGH FASTING

Fasting is another way to achieve intimacy with God. The purpose of fasting is not to gain God's favor. You don't need to gain God's favor, because He already loves you, and He will never love you any more than He loves you right now. In scripture there are examples of people who fasted in order to receive an answer to prayer, but the greatest purpose of fasting isn't to get your prayers answered, rather it is a way to obtain greater intimacy with God.

Yeshua was questioned as to why His disciples didn't fast. He responded that they didn't need to fast, because the bridegroom was still with them, but when the bridegroom was taken away, then they would fast. Yeshua is the bridegroom, and His disciples would be fasting for intimacy and fellowship with Him after His departure from them.

> [14]*Then John's disciples came and asked him, "How is it that we and the Pharisees fast, but your disciples do not fast?"* [15]*Jesus answered, "How can the guests of the bridegroom mourn while he is with them? The time*

will come when the bridegroom will be taken from them; then they will fast." ~Matthew 9:14-15 NIV

Fasting makes you thirsty and hungry for God. When you fast, you will look to God, alone, as your source for life. As you recognize your sole dependence upon Him, a greater focus and clarity will evolve in your life, drawing you into greater intimacy with Him. When you fast, don't think that you're going to have some cosmic experience or think that when the fast is over that everything in your life will be perfect. It's not true. I have fasted significantly, and when the fast was finished, frankly, I was a little discouraged, because I had hoped more would happen.

Several years ago, I had prayed for an entire year asking God for greater peace in my life. After one year, the LORD came to me in a dream one night. In the dream, I found myself in a dense, green forest. The forest was totally surrounded with rock formations covered with lush ivy, making the forest a secret, secluded paradise. It was by far the lushest, greenest forest I had ever seen or experienced.

As I encountered the beauty of this forest, the Spirit of God came over me in billows of peace. God kept filling me with His presence and peace, as He led me deeper and deeper into the forest. Deep within the forest, I saw a simple wooden picnic table. I believe that this picnic table represented the fullness of God's peace. I felt the Spirit of God drawing me deeper into the forest towards this picnic table. As the Spirit of God was drawing me deeper into the forest towards the picnic table, I suddenly smelled pizza in my dream. The smell of the pizza was so strong that it made me hungry, even though I wasn't hungry before I smelled it.

I didn't know what to do. On one hand, I wanted to follow the Spirit of God deeper into the forest towards the picnic table to experience more of His presence and peace, but on the other hand, I desired to have the pizza. I wanted both! Then I thought to myself, "Maybe I could have a piece of pizza and then follow God's Spirit deeper into the forest." As soon as that thought came into my mind, the dream was over. I was so grieved! This encounter with the LORD was one of the most incredible and emotionally satisfying experiences I have ever had, and I traded it for a lousy piece of pizza.

I got out of bed and fell on my knees and cried out, "LORD, forgive me. I can't believe I did that. I've been praying for an entire year for Your peace in my life, and I traded it for a lousy piece of pizza. Please give me another chance."

I went back to bed hoping I would fall back asleep and that the LORD would visit me again, but it didn't happen. In the morning when I awoke, I was so grieved. I asked the LORD, "Why did this happen? Did Satan steal Your peace from me? Where did the pizza come from? Did you bring it to me, or was it Satan trying to rob me of what You wanted to give me?" Then I thought, "But LORD, even if it was Satan, I still believe that you engineered the entire dream." Next, the LORD spoke to me saying, "If you'll deny yourself the natural, then you'll be drawn deeper into the supernatural, and you'll experience more of My glory and peace."

Through fasting, in denying yourself the natural, you will experience more of God's supernatural. Fasting draws you into greater intimacy and oneness with Him, but this desired intimacy and oneness won't come in a single day or a month; it will take a lifetime.

Yeshua expects you to live a life of fasting. He didn't say, if you fast, but rather, "when you fast."

> [16]*"When you fast, do not look somber as the hypocrites do, for they disfigure their faces to show men they*

are fasting. I tell you the truth, they have received their reward in full. ¹⁷*But when you fast, put oil on your head and wash your face,* ¹⁸*so that it will not be obvious to men that you are fasting, but only to your Father, who is unseen; and your Father, who sees what is done in secret, will reward you." -Matthew 6:16-18 NIV*

I had always romanced about fasting, envisioning myself fasting 40 days and 40 nights in the woods. Years ago, I decided to go on such a fast. A friend of mine let me use his cabin in Kentucky for the fast. I drove all the way down to the cabin and started the fast, but after just 32 hours, my hunger overcame me, and I ended up driving to McDonald's to eat.

I had never been able to successfully complete a fast. Every time I tried to fast, I failed, but now after receiving this dream from the LORD, I felt an imparted power within me to be able to successfully complete a fast. With that imparted power, I started my fast.

For the first 21 days of the fast, I ate only one meal a day. Then for the next 19 days, I had no food at all, and finally the last three days, I had no food or water, whatsoever. When the fast was over, I was extremely thin and emaciated. I looked very sickly. Even Yeshua, after He had completed His fast, needed angels to come and minister to Him.

> ¹¹*Then the devil left Him; and behold, angels came and began to minister to Him. -Matthew 4:11 NASB*

I had great expectations of my fast, but when it was over, it seemed as if nothing had changed in my life. But the reality is, things had changed. God had done a transforming work in me, even though it was different than what I anticipated. Fasting, beloved, done in the right way, changes us. God uses it to transform us and to gain possession of us for Himself. You may not necessarily experience bliss as a result of fasting, but as you rely on God to be your only source, you will be drawn into greater intimacy with Him, and over time, your passion for intimacy with Him will be realized.

3. CULTIVATING INTIMACY THROUGH LEES POG

Lees pog is a Hebrew word which means *to soak up.* When you spend time in *lees pog*, you are simply sitting before the LORD, resting and soaking in His presence, not striving to do anything.

The culture we live in today is one of constant busyness. Our lives are busy doing so many things. Oftentimes, we even overburden ourselves in the pursuit of spiritual things. We believe that if we do more, then we'll become more, but we must recognize that we are human *beings* not human *doings*.

Many of you need to come out of the busy lifestyles you've been leading. If you truly desire to cultivate intimacy with God, you need to spend time every day with Him.

David, the king of Israel, found intimacy with the LORD, simply by spending time resting in His presence.

²Surely I have composed and quieted my soul; Like a weaned child rests against his mother, My soul is like a weaned child within me. ~Psalm 131:2 NASB

It is interesting to note that David is the one individual whom Yeshua is most clearly linked to in the Hebrew Bible (Old Testament). Yeshua testified that He is the offspring of David.

> [16]*"I, Jesus, have sent my angel to give you this testimony for the churches. I am the Root and the Offspring of David, and the bright Morning Star." ~Revelation 22:16 NIV*

David took time every day seeking the LORD, resting in Him, and he became the man he was because of it. What did David know about this concept of resting in the LORD? He speaks about it in Psalm 23. He describes how the LORD made him lie down and be still, and as he did, the LORD restored his soul. David's soul became refreshed, as he rested in the LORD.

> [1]*The LORD is my shepherd, I shall not be in want.* [2]*He makes me lie down in green pastures, he leads me beside quiet waters,* [3]*he restores my soul. ~Psalm 23:1-3a NIV*

The LORD, Himself, demonstrates for us the importance of this concept of resting. The book of Genesis speaks of how God worked six days creating all of His creation, and then He rested from His work on the seventh day (Sabbath). He blessed the Sabbath Day and made it holy (set apart).

> [2]*By the seventh day God had finished the work he had been doing; so on the seventh day he rested from all his work.* [3]*And God blessed the seventh day and made it holy, because on it he rested from all the work of creating that he had done. ~Genesis 2:2-3 NIV*

The LORD didn't need to rest, because He never becomes tired; He instead was showing us a pattern for our own lives of how we should work six days and rest on the seventh.

Yeshua also spoke about the importance of rest. He told us the Sabbath was made for man and not man for the Sabbath.

> [27] *Then he said to them, "The Sabbath was made for man, not man for the Sabbath." ~Mark 2:27 NIV*

The word Sabbath means *to rest*. Resting is a creation principle designed by God. He built into our lives the need to rest. If we attempt to work seven days a week, without a day of rest, we will burn out and be very ineffective in our lives, but if we follow God's example of resting one day a week, we will be blessed as He refreshes and restores us.

Just as we need to rest one day a week, we also need to set apart a certain amount of time each day to rest in the LORD's presence to be refreshed. David in Psalm 131:2 compared his resting in the LORD to that of a weaned child resting on its mother's bosom. David wasn't working or striving. He was simply being still and quiet, and in that stillness and quietness, he found contentment and nourishment in his relationship with God. How many of us understand this concept? God, oftentimes, wants us to understand that He's not asking us to do something for Him but rather to simply receive from Him. We don't need to become better *doers*; we need to become better *receivers*.

Many of us think receiving is a one-time thing. There is an initial receiving of Messiah, but we need to receive Him every day, all day long, just like the air we breathe. If we stop breathing air, we will die, and if we aren't receiving Messiah daily, we will die spiritually. We need to continually receive Him with a greater and greater capacity, and when we do, the person of Yeshua and His power will manifest through our lives.

Many believers are so busy reading spiritual books or doing things for the LORD that they haven't come to the place where they just simply sit before Him. As you begin to sit before Him, He will enlarge your capacity to receive from Him. He will increase your ability to focus and meditate on Him, and He will enhance your ability to sense the leading of the Holy Spirit.

Many of you are engaging in so many daily activities that it becomes difficult to place yourself every day in a position of receiving from God. It is important for you to take time each day to be still before God, allowing Him to speak to you.

When you desire to communicate something important to someone, you don't attempt to communicate it when that person's attention is on something else; instead you wait until their focus is entirely on you. The LORD communicates to us in the same manner. He won't communicate something to us, until our focus is entirely upon Him.

My hope is that you will make a lifetime commitment to spend time every day with the LORD, so He can communicate His truth into your life. It's not about being busy or doing more, it's simply about sitting before Him and receiving from Him, and when you do, His presence will flow from you. It will be a natural overflow of having communion with Him. Over time, He will manifest Himself to you in greater ways than ever before, and you will literally fall in love with Him.

Chapter Three

Sharing Yeshua With Jewish People

GOD'S CALL ON YOUR LIFE

In this chapter, I will lay a scriptural foundation to help you understand that God has a specific call on your life, as a believer, to reach the Jewish people with the Good News of Yeshua. In so doing, I hope to help you better understand God's heart for the Jewish community and His plan to use you to reach them. I will share with you some aspects of Jewish culture to help you identify with them, as well as suggest some specific strategies which will help you in witnessing. Lastly, I will share several theological objections Jewish people have concerning Yeshua and will respond to these objections, equipping you to help them see the truth of the scriptures.

God has placed a call on every believer to share the message of Yeshua HaMashiach with people from every tribe, tongue, and nation.

[8]"and you will be my witnesses in Jerusalem, and in all Judea and Samaria, and to the ends of the earth."
~Acts 1:8b NIV

The Bible divides humanity into two classes of people: the Jews and the Gentiles. The term "the Gentiles" is most often used to designate all people who are not Jewish (or of the 12 Tribes of Israel). Scripturally, we are commanded to preach the Gospel to all people groups of the world, but God specifically instructs us to reach out to the Jews first.

[16]I am not ashamed of the gospel, because it is the power of God for the salvation of everyone who believes: first for the Jew, then for the Gentile. ~Romans 1:16 NIV

When I'm ministering to various congregations, I've noticed they sometimes have a special wall dedicated to the missionaries they support. Praise God, these missionaries are sharing the Gospel with many nations around the world. It shocks me, however, that sometimes they are supporting thirty different missionaries, yet, not one of them is to the nation of Israel.

Even though Yeshua came for all people, He spoke specifically of His coming for the nation of Israel.

[24]He answered, "I was sent only to the lost sheep of Israel."
~Matthew 15:24 NIV

When the apostle Paul (Shaul) went on his missionary journeys, he always went to the synagogue first to share the Good News of the Kingdom with the Jews before going to the Gentiles. It was the Jews who first brought the Gospel message to the Gentiles, and now God desires to use the Gentiles to bring the message of Yeshua back to the Jews.

THE ROMANS ROAD

Many of you have heard the term the *Romans Road*. It is an evangelistic term describing how the book of Romans can be used to lead a person into a relationship with God. The *Romans Road* shows that we are all sinners and that the penalty for sin is death, but God in His mercy sent His Son, Yeshua, to pay our penalty for sin and save us. This is all very true, of course, but to more fully understand the book of Romans, we need to know what was in the heart of Paul (Shaul), its author, when he wrote it. We will be examining that in this chapter.

SHAUL'S AWAKENING

Shaul wrote most of the New Testament. He was one of the great Jewish leaders of his day, educated under the distinguished teacher, Gamaliel. Shaul was from the tribe of Benjamin, and he lived as a Pharisee. He was enraged by any Jew who confessed Yeshua to be the Messiah and was zealous in persecuting them.

In fact, there was a Jew named Stephen, who confessed Yeshua to be the Messiah, and because of his faith, the traditional Jewish community stoned him to death. Shaul not only watched the stoning, but he was in hearty agreement with it. He continually imprisoned and persecuted many Jews who confessed Yeshua to be the Messiah.

In his zealousness, Shaul obtained permission from the religious leaders in Jerusalem to travel to Damascus, a city approximately 140 miles north of Jerusalem, to arrest any Jew there who believed in Yeshua. While traveling to Damascus, Yeshua supernaturally appeared to him as a bright light from heaven. As the brightness flashed around him, Shaul instantly fell to the ground and was immediately blinded.

> [1] *Meanwhile, Saul was still breathing out murderous threats against the Lord's disciples. He went to the high priest* [2] *and asked him for letters to the synagogues in Damascus, so that if he found any there who belonged to the Way, whether men or women, he might take them as prisoners to Jerusalem.* [3] *As he neared Damascus on his journey, suddenly a light from heaven flashed around him.* [4] *He fell to the ground and heard a voice say to him, "Saul, Saul, why do you persecute me?"* [5] *"Who are you, Lord?" Saul asked. "I am Jesus, whom you are persecuting," he replied.* [6] *"Now get up and go into the city, and you will be told what you must do."*
> *~Acts 9:1-6 NIV*

Following this supernatural vision, Shaul became a believer in Yeshua, and today, he is regarded as the most influential preacher and evangelist the world has ever known.

SHAUL'S LONGING DESIRE

Although the book of Romans includes the road map to salvation, it contains much, much more. A large portion of the book reveals God's plan to bring the Jewish people to faith through the Gentiles and explains that Israel's coming to faith will usher in Yeshua's return.

We need to read Romans through the heart of its writer, Shaul, who desperately wanted to see Jewish people come to faith in Yeshua. The entire chapter of Romans 9 is about Shaul's longing desire to see Israel saved. This longing desire is not only his, but it is also that of the Holy Spirit. If you are a believer and you love God, let the Holy Spirit touch you with His love for the Jewish people, a love that will give you a passion to reach them with the Good News of Yeshua.

Shaul had such an intense sorrow for the masses of Jewish people, who were rejecting Yeshua, that he was willing to give up his own salvation to see them saved. It's like a father who says to his son or daughter that he would be willing to cut off his own hand, if it would help them.

> *¹I speak the truth in (Messiah)—I am not lying, my conscience confirms it in the Holy Spirit— ²I have great sorrow and unceasing anguish in my heart. ³For I could wish that I myself were cursed and cut off from (Messiah) for the sake of my brothers, those of my own race, ⁴the people of Israel. ~Romans 9:1-4a NIV*

Shaul begins Romans 10 in the same way, with a passionate plea for the salvation of Israel. He laments because so many Jewish people have not come to faith in Yeshua.

> *¹Brothers, my heart's desire and prayer to God for the Israelites is that they may be saved. ~Romans 10:1 NIV*

As you can now see, the book of Romans is more than a road map to personal salvation, it is also about the salvation of Israel. Shaul continues his plea for the salvation of Israel in Romans 11. He tells us that God is not done with the Jewish people, even though most of them have stumbled over Yeshua and rejected Him. He explains they haven't fallen forever, because God has a plan in all of it. His plan is to bring salvation to the Gentiles, who, in return, will provoke the Jews to jealousy, and in their jealousy, the Jews will come to faith.

> *¹I ask then: Did God reject his people? By no means! I am an Israelite myself, a descendant of Abraham, from the tribe of Benjamin. ²God did not reject his people, whom he foreknew. ~Romans 11:1-2 NIV*

> [11]*Again I ask: Did they stumble so as to fall beyond recovery? Not at all! Rather, because of their transgression, salvation has come to the Gentiles to make Israel envious.* ~Romans 11:11 NIV

Isn't this an awesome thing? God starts out revealing Himself to the Jews, and then He uses the Jews to bring salvation to the Gentiles, who then bring salvation back to the Jews.

> [33]*Oh the depth of the riches of the wisdom and knowledge of God! How unsearchable his judgments, and his paths beyond tracing out!* [34]*"Who has known the mind of the Lord? Or who has been his counselor?"* [35]*"Who has ever given to God, that God should repay him?"* [36]*For from him and through him and to him are all things. To him be the glory forever! Amen.* ~Romans 11:33-36 NIV

So you can now see, if you are a Gentile believer, God has placed a princely and specific call on your life; the call to reach the Jewish people with the Good News of Yeshua.

SHAUL – APOSTLE TO THE GENTILES

After Shaul received the vision of Yeshua, he went back to the Temple, believing God would release him to witness to his Jewish brethren. He may have thought to himself, "Who else would be a better witness than me, a Pharisee who has previously persecuted Jews for their faith in Yeshua? They will believe me, when I proclaim to them that Yeshua is their Messiah, because I once persecuted those who believed in Yeshua." But contrary to what Shaul might have thought, God sent him far away to witness to the Gentiles, because the Jews were not going to accept his testimony. In Acts 22, Yeshua speaks to Shaul saying:

> [18]*"Leave Jerusalem immediately, because they will not accept your testimony about me."... [21]Then the Lord said to me, "Go; I will send you far away to the Gentiles." -Acts 22:18b, 21 NIV*

PROVOKING THE JEWS TO JEALOUSY

The result of the Jewish people rejecting the message of Yeshua is that it then came to the Gentiles. Shaul became an apostle to the Gentiles, and as he shared the Gospel throughout the world, many Gentiles were saved. He magnified his ministry to the Gentiles, because he understood God's plan to reach the Jewish people through the witness of Gentile believers. As a result of the Gentiles coming to faith, the Jews would be provoked to jealousy and thus come to faith themselves.

> [11]*salvation has come to the Gentiles to make Israel envious -Romans 11:11b NIV*

> [13]*Inasmuch as I am the apostle to the Gentiles, I make much of my ministry [14]in the hope that I may somehow arouse my own people to envy and save some of them. -Romans 11:13b-14 NIV*

Shaul explains to the Gentile believers that if they were blessed when the Jewish people rejected the Gospel, how much more blessed will they be when the Jewish people receive it? He tells them it will be, "life from the dead."

**¹⁵*For if their rejection is the reconciliation of the world, what will their acceptance be but life from the dead?*
~Romans 11:15 NIV

Shaul is literally speaking of the resurrection from the dead when Yeshua returns.

GOD'S OLIVE TREE

God uses the illustration of an olive tree in Romans 11 to reveal His great plan to us that encompasses both Jews and Gentiles. The olive tree was originally all Jewish, but when many Jewish people rejected Yeshua, some of the natural (Jewish) branches were broken off. In God's lovingkindness, He grafted in branches from a wild olive tree (the Gentiles).

Since the Gentiles have now come into the family of God, Shaul tells them they should not be prideful or arrogant towards the Jews for not believing, because just as the natural (Jewish) branches were broken off for their unbelief, so, too, God can break off the grafted (Gentile) branches for their arrogance. If God can do what is contrary to nature by grafting wild (Gentile) branches into an olive tree, He surely will have no difficulty grafting the natural (Jewish) branches back into the tree, when they finally come to faith in Yeshua.

¹⁷If some of the branches have been broken off, and you, though a wild olive shoot, have been grafted in among the others and now share in the nourishing sap from the olive root, ¹⁸do not boast over those branches. If you do, consider this: You do not support the root, but the root supports you. ¹⁹You will say then, "Branches were broken off so that I could be grafted in." ²⁰Granted. But they were broken off because of unbelief, and you stand by faith. Do not be arrogant, but be afraid. ²¹For if God

87

*did not spare the natural branches, he will not spare you
either. ²²Consider therefore the kindness and sternness
of God: sternness to those who fell, but kindness to you,
provided that you continue in his kindness. Otherwise,
you also will be cut off. ²³And if they do not persist in
unbelief, they will be grafted in, for God is able to graft
them in again. ²⁴After all, if you were cut out of an olive
tree that is wild by nature, and contrary to nature were
grafted into a cultivated olive tree, how much more
readily will these, the natural branches, be grafted into
their own olive tree! ~Romans 11:17-24 NIV*

GENTILES — GRAFTED INTO THE COMMONWEALTH OF ISRAEL

Every covenant God made, He made with the Jewish
people, and the Gentiles are grafted into those covenants,
according to the promise He made with Abraham.

*¹⁸"In your seed all the nations of the earth shall be
blessed," ~Genesis 22:18a NASB*

*¹⁶Now the promises were spoken to Abraham and to
his seed. He does not say, "And to seeds," as referring
to many, but rather to one, "And to your seed," that is,
(Messiah). ~Galatians 3:16 NASB*

*¹⁴in order that in (Messiah) Jesus the blessing of
Abraham might come to the Gentiles, so that we
would receive the promise of the Spirit through faith.
~Galatians 3:14 NASB*

Yeshua is the offspring of Abraham, and it is through Him
that the Gentiles have been grafted into the commonwealth

of Israel. Every Gentile, who has a relationship with the God of Israel, has this relationship through Yeshua.

> [11]*Therefore, remember that formerly you who are Gentiles by birth and called "uncircumcised" by those who call themselves "the circumcision" (that done in the body by the hands of men)—* [12]*remember that at that time you were separate from (Messiah), excluded from citizenship in Israel and foreigners to the covenants of the promise, without hope and without God in the world.* [13]*But now in (Messiah) Jesus, you who once were far away have been brought near through the blood of (Messiah). ~Ephesians 2:11-13 NIV*

USHERING IN YESHUA'S RETURN

Shaul shares with us a mystery as to why most Jews have not yet accepted the Gospel message. The mystery is that Israel has experienced a partial spiritual hardening which will last for a divinely specified period of time. This time of spiritual hardening will end when Gentile believers come into the fullness of their calling, both in numbers and in their acceptance of their role to reach Jewish people. As Gentiles share their faith with Jewish people, the Jews will come to faith, and they will call upon Yeshua HaMashiach to return, ushering in His glorious coming. Hallelujah!

> [25]*I do not want you to be ignorant of this mystery, brothers, so that you may not be conceited: Israel has experienced a hardening in part until the full number of the Gentiles has come in.* [26]*And so all Israel will be saved, as it is written: "The deliverer will come from Zion; he will turn godlessness away from Jacob.* [27]*And*

this is my covenant with them when I take away their sins." ~Romans 11:25-27 NIV

Yeshua said He would not return again until a mass of Jewish people are crying out to Him, saying, "Blessed is He who comes in the name of the LORD." (In Hebrew: "Baruch haba b'shem Adonai.")

³⁹*"For I tell you, you will not see me again until you say, 'Blessed is he who comes in the name of the Lord.'"* *~Matthew 23:39 NIV*

Yeshua is going to use his bride's cry for His return to prepare the spiritual atmosphere for His coming. He will return in response to the call of His bride. He will use the prayers of His people to usher in His return. This is why Revelation 22:17 says,

¹⁷*The Spirit and the bride say, "Come!" ~Revelation 22:17a NIV*

²⁰*"Yes, I am coming soon." Amen. Come, Lord Jesus. ~Revelation 22:20b NIV*

I pray that you have a natural love for the Jewish people, but even if you don't, it is to your advantage to be active in bringing the Good News to them, because their coming to faith plays a key role in ushering in Yeshua's return!

FULFILLING YOUR CALL

I know some of you may never have an opportunity to personally share your faith in Yeshua with a Jewish person, even though I pray many of you will. For those of you who may never get an opportunity, you can still fulfill your call to reach Jewish people through your prayers and your financial support. It's possible that some of you may never have a direct witnessing opportunity to a Jewish person, but by financially supporting ministries like this one, you will share with and have a part in equipping those who will. Additionally, by financially supporting this ministry, you are helping to broadcast the message of Yeshua HaMashiach to Jewish people throughout the world, even into Israel.

BEING ALL THINGS TO ALL PEOPLE

Shaul knew, in order to reach the person he was witnessing to, he would have to adapt his approach specifically to that person. He knew he would need to be all things to all men. To the Jew, he became as a Jew; to the Gentile, he became as a Gentile. He adapted his approach so he could reach all mankind, whether Jew or Gentile.

> [20]*To the Jews I became like a Jew, to win the Jews. To those under the law I became like one under the law (though I myself am not under the law), so as to win those under the law.* [21]*To those not having the law I became like one not having the law (though I am not free from God's law but am under [Messiah's] law), so as to win those not having the law.* [22]*To the weak I became weak, to win the weak. I have become all things to all men so that by all possible means I might save some.* -I Corinthians 9:20-22 NIV*

UNDERSTANDING JEWISH CULTURE

Just as Shaul adapted his approach specifically for each person, you, too, will need to do the same when witnessing to Jewish people. As I share with you some aspects of Jewish culture, I pray it will help you better understand them, equipping you to become a better witness.

1. JEWISH PEOPLE ARE EDUCATIONALLY MINDED

There is a high emphasis in the Jewish home on education and a desire to see their children become successful. Oftentimes, in the Jewish community, you will hear the saying, "my son, the doctor" or "my son, the lawyer." It is a fact that Jewish people win more Nobel prizes proportionately than any other people group on earth, and this is partly due to their emphasis on education.

2. JEWISH PEOPLE HAVE A HIGH PRIORITY ON FAMILY

Jewish people have a high priority on family, and their families are very closely knit. Although they do have problems, just like other families, studies show there is less divorce, alcoholism, incest, drug addictions, etc. In addition to having strong family units, Jewish people tend to stick together in general. Some Gentiles have been offended with this, seeing them as clannish; in reality, this is how they have been able to survive and prosper in a world that is 99% non-Jewish. Jewish people tend to do business with other Jewish people, live in predominately Jewish neighborhoods, marry within their faith, and develop their most intimate friendships with other Jews. This, however, is changing as the world is becoming more open-minded and diverse.

3. MANY JEWISH PEOPLE ARE SECULAR

When Gentiles see Jews dressed in black praying at the Western Wall, they mistakenly believe that all Jews are religious. The reality is that most Jews are secular. Being Jewish, for most Jews, has little to do with being religious or defining their beliefs; rather, it is a cultural identity for them. Even those who attend synagogue, oftentimes, are not educated about the Hebrew Bible. Instead, they are taught traditions and rabbinic teachings. Many Bible-believing Christians know the Hebrew Bible better than most Jewish people.

4. JEWISH PEOPLE ARE SEARCHING FOR GOD

God has given Jewish people a natural tendency to search for Him. Because traditional Judaism doesn't satisfy their hunger for God, many Jews have been drawn to the New Age religion and other false cults. Oftentimes, you can provoke a Jew to jealousy when you speak to them about a God who has a personal relationship with you, who answers your prayers, who is your friend, and who loves you. This is what Shaul meant in Romans 11:11 when he said:

[11]*salvation has come to the Gentiles to make Israel envious. ~Romans 11:11b NIV*

5. JEWS BELIEVE THEY
CANNOT BE A JEW AND A CHRISTIAN

Jewish people mistakenly believe they can no longer be Jewish, if they become a *Christian*. They fail to understand that Yeshua didn't come to start a new religion called *Christianity*. He simply is the fulfillment of Judaism.

When a Jewish person accepts Yeshua as the Messiah, he or she is not converting to some other religion called *Christianity*. The word *Christianity* is not even found in the New Testament. It was developed by the church fathers in an effort to distinguish the doctrines of faith contained in the New Testament from the other religions of the world, but it is not a biblical term.

The word *Christian* is found in the Bible three times, but it isn't used to designate a different religion from Judaism. A *Christian* simply is a follower of the Anointed One. The word for the Anointed One in Hebrew is Mashiach or in the Greek, Christ. When the Bible uses the word *Christian*, it speaks of one, whether Jew or Gentile, who is following the Anointed One.

So, when a Jew embraces Yeshua as the Messiah, he is not changing religions; he is simply embracing the Anointed One, Yeshua HaMashiach, who has fulfilled Judaism. So, again, the term Christian, then, does not imply whether one is a Jew or a Gentile, but rather designates that one is following Yeshua HaMashiach, Jesus the Christ, the Anointed One.

6. JEWS PERSECUTE OTHER
JEWS WHO BELIEVE IN YESHUA

Not only do the vast majority of Jewish people today not recognize Yeshua as the Messiah, but Jews who do profess faith in Him are often frowned upon and ostracized by the larger Jewish community.

Ever since Israel was created as the Jewish homeland, Jewish people can move to Israel from anywhere in the world and become Israeli citizens. You can be a Jew who doesn't believe in God and be granted citizenship. You can be a Jew who believes in the New Age movement and be granted citizenship. There is only one type of Jew who has been discriminated against and denied citizenship; that is a Jew who claims Yeshua to be the Messiah. Only recently has the law prohibiting Messianic Jews from gaining Israeli citizenship been changed.

Most Jews today don't know why they are so prejudiced against Jews who believe in Yeshua or why they are so resistant to Him themselves. When you ask a Jewish person why they don't believe in Yeshua, many will say something like, "Well, I don't know. I'm a Jew, and Jesus isn't for Jews." That's their only explanation.

7. MANY JEWISH PEOPLE HAVE AN ANTI-YESHUA MINDSET

Many Jewish people have been brought up to have an anti-Yeshua mindset. This anti-Yeshua mindset has been passed down from one generation of Jews to the next and can be traced all the way back to the Pharisees of Yeshua's day. These Pharisees hated Yeshua, because He exposed them as hypocrites. Yeshua described them as whitewashed tombstones. They appeared brilliantly white and clean-looking on the outside but were actually corrupt and dirty on the inside.

[27]*"Woe to you, teachers of the law and Pharisees, you hypocrites! You are like whitewashed tombs, which look*

> *beautiful on the outside but on the inside are full of*
> *dead men's bones and everything unclean." ~Matthew*
> *23:27 NIV*

Modern day rabbinic Judaism has its origin in the sons of these Pharisees that Yeshua condemned. In 70 CE (Common Era), the Romans destroyed the Temple in Jerusalem because of Jewish resistance to the Roman ways. When the Romans invaded Jerusalem and destroyed the Temple, everything changed in the Jewish religious world. With no Temple, there could be no sacrifices; without a Temple and sacrifices, there could be no Priesthood. This collapse of the Temple, the Priesthood, and the sacrificial system, as described in the Torah, dealt a catastrophic blow to "Biblical Judaism."

In other words, the Judaism of the Bible, in many ways, could no longer be followed. For example, the book of Leviticus tells the Israelites that on Yom Kippur (the Day of Atonement), a blood sacrifice had to be offered to Yahweh by the High Priest of Israel. Without a Temple, Priesthood, or sacrifices, this could no longer be done. As a result, Judaism had to be redefined. This redefinition of Judaism took place in 90 CE at the Council of Yavneh. The participants in this critical Council were none other than the sons of the Pharisees who were largely behind Yeshua's execution.

> [47]*Then the chief priests and the Pharisees called a meeting of the Sanhedrin. "What are we accomplishing?" they asked. "Here is this man performing many miraculous signs."…* [53]*So from that day on they plotted to take his life. ~John 11:47,53 NIV*

These Pharisees hated Yeshua, because they were losing their influence with the people. Many Jews began to follow Yeshua, instead of these Pharisees, who were accustomed to being Israel's religious leaders. The Pharisees response to losing their power was to kill Yeshua. No doubt, this anti-Yeshua mindset was passed down to these Pharisees' sons who redefined Judaism at the Council of Yavneh. As I stated, modern day Judaism is traced back to this Council; as a result, there is within the Judaism of today this anti-Yeshua mentality. So, today, Jews reject Jesus without even knowing that their rejection of Him has been passed on to them by the corrupt Pharisees of Yeshua's day.

8. SOME JEWS BELIEVE CHRISTIANS ARE ANTI-SEMITIC

Just as Gentiles may make the mistake of thinking all Jews are alike, Jews sometimes mistakenly believe all Gentiles are Christians and are anti-Semitic.

The Jewish people have been one of the most mistreated ethnic groups in the entire world. They have endured persecution for thousands of years, all energized by Satan and much of it done in the name of Christianity.

In general, the Jewish community perceives anti-Semitism as being linked to Christianity. A Jewish person once said to me, "It's not Jesus I'm rejecting; it's what He stands for." Because Jewish people have suffered persecution in the name of Christianity, when they think of Jesus, they think of anti-Semitism.

For almost 2,000 years, Christians have persecuted Jews and called them the Christ killers. Historians tell us that the murder of six million Jews in the holocaust could never have happened, unless there had already been tremendous anti-Semitism, not only in the world, but in the church. The Nazi holocaust was so brutal that German soldiers actually took Jewish babies, threw them in the air, and shot and killed them for target practice in front of their parents. They would then look at the parents and say, "That's because you're the Christ killers." Hitler's picture was even hung in many churches throughout Europe during the Nazi holocaust.

The Jewish people also encountered persecution from Christians during the many years of the Crusades. One historical fact that isn't well known is that in 1492, it wasn't only Columbus who sailed the ocean blue; the Jews were also sailing on the ocean. Ferdinand and Isabella had issued an edict expelling all 200,000 Jews from Spain. Many Jews paid Spanish ship captains exorbitant sums of money to sail them to other countries; but instead of being taken to the other countries, they were dumped overboard in the middle of the ocean to drown. There were tens of thousands of other Jews who died fleeing Spain, because many countries refused to receive them.

The Jewish people have also endured anti-Semitism from Christians who have embraced the concept of replacement theology. Replacement theology states that because Israel has rejected Yeshua, God has taken from them His covenant promises and has given them to the church. It also states that the Jewish people are no longer God's chosen people, but that the church has replaced them as His chosen ones. Christian anti-Semitism has grown in the church over the last 1,900 years from this false teaching. It's no wonder that Jewish people have come to believe that Christians are anti-Semitic.

9. MOST JEWISH PEOPLE ARE NOT WAITING FOR A MESSIAH

Even though the Hebrew prophets foretold of numerous prophecies about a coming Messiah, in reality, many, if not most, Jewish people today are not literally waiting for a Messiah to come. Some are waiting for a messianic age, a time of peace on earth; others have lost hope all together. During the time of the prophets, the people of Israel waited in great anticipation for the Messiah's coming. The prophet, Isaiah, prophesied that the people would rejoice in the salvation that Messiah would bring, after waiting upon Him to come.

> [9]*And it will be said in that day, "Behold, this is our God for whom we have waited that He might save us. This is the LORD for whom we have waited; Let us rejoice and be glad in His salvation." ~Isaiah 25:9 NASB*

Isaiah also prophesied of one who would come before Messiah, preparing the way for His coming.

> [3]*A voice of one calling: "In the desert prepare the way for the LORD; make straight in the wilderness a highway for our God.* [4]*Every valley shall be raised up, every mountain and hill made low; the rough ground shall become level, the rugged places a plain.* [5]*And the glory of the LORD will be revealed, and all mankind together will see it. For the mouth of the LORD has spoken." ~Isaiah 40:3-5 NIV*

When John the Baptist came upon the scene in Judea, he called for the people of Israel to repent of their sins, thus preparing their hearts for the coming of Messiah. The people were in great anticipation of Messiah's coming and wondered if John was indeed the Messiah. John told the people that he immersed them with water, but One would come later, who would immerse them with the Holy Spirit and with fire.

> ¹⁵*The people were waiting expectantly and were all wondering in their hearts if John might possibly be the (Messiah). ¹⁶John answered them all, "I baptize you with water. But one more powerful than I will come, the thongs of whose sandals I am not worthy to untie. He will baptize you with the Holy Spirit and with fire." ~Luke 3:15-16 NIV*

There was a righteous man in Jerusalem named Simeon who eagerly awaited the Messiah's coming. The Holy Spirit had revealed to him that he would not see death, until he had seen the coming Messiah. This promise was fulfilled, when Simeon saw Yeshua, when He was brought to the Temple by His parents. (Luke 2:25-35)

There also was a prophetess in Jerusalem named Anna, who had long awaited for the Messiah to come. She was a widow, and she had been praying and fasting, night and day, over a period of 77 years for the coming of Messiah, never leaving the Temple. Her prayers finally were answered, when she saw the Messiah the day He was brought to the Temple. (Luke 2:36-38)

As I said earlier, most Jewish people today are not looking for a personal Messiah; some are looking for a messianic age and others have lost hope in a Messiah completely. In the 12th century, however, there was a Jewish philosopher and rabbi named Maimonides who developed the 13 Articles of the Jewish Faith. These articles of faith are widely accepted today as a proper expression of the Jewish faith and still appear in Jewish prayer books.

Although Maimonides rejected Yeshua as the Messiah, He did include in his codification of Judaism the coming of a personal Messiah to the Jewish people. The 12th article of the Jewish Faith by Maimonides says, "The Messiah will come." It states, "I believe with perfect faith in the coming of the Messiah; and even though he may tarry, nonetheless, I wait every day for his coming." Maimonides, who codified Judaism, believed that Messiah would come as a person instead of a messianic age. The point is that, historically, the Jewish people have believed in the coming of a personal Messiah, not a messianic age.

It seems obvious that our world is not evolving into a messianic age of peace. With the proliferation of nuclear weapons, the economy spiraling downward, divorce rates climbing, and moral decay on the increase, it is hard to envision that we are moving toward some utopian messianic age.

The apostle, Shaul, speaks in Romans 8 of how the earth is decaying and how it waits in anticipation of Messiah to come.

> *[19]The creation waits in eager expectation for the sons of God to be revealed. [20]For the creation was subjected to frustration, not by its own choice, but by the will of the one who subjected it, in hope [21]that the creation itself will be liberated from its bondage to decay and brought into the glorious freedom of the children of God. [22]We know that the whole creation has been groaning as in the pains of childbirth right up to the present time.*
> *~Romans 8:19-22 NIV*

The increase in earthquakes and other natural disasters we've experienced in recent years is evidence of this. Yeshua referred to this in Matthew 24:7-8, when He said:

> *[7]"There will be famines and earthquakes in various places. [8]All these are the beginning of birth pains."*
> *~Matthew 24:7b-8 NIV*

101

Expecting and waiting for a messianic age of peace to evolve out of this dark and evil world is not reality. Yeshua HaMashiach is the only answer! Jewish people need to know that Yeshua is the Messiah, who has already come and is coming again to bring peace to the world. He came the first time to die in our place, as a sacrifice for our sin. (Isaiah 53) He's coming back a second time to be King and to rule the world in peace. How will they know that Yeshua is their Messiah, unless we tell them?

WITNESSING STRATEGIES

Yahweh desires for Gentile believers to understand His heart for Israel. He wants to inspire, train, and mobilize Gentiles to be His missionaries and ambassadors to the Jewish people. Whether it is a friend, neighbor, coworker, or someone you unexpectedly meet, He wants you to be able to effectively witness to them about Yeshua.

This next section contains numerous witnessing strategies. Although these strategies focus on witnessing to Jewish people, they can just as easily be used when sharing your faith with Gentiles. It is my prayer that as you put them into practice, the Holy Spirit will open the eyes, minds, and hearts of those you are witnessing to, and many will come to know Yeshua!

1. BEING OBEDIENT IN THE MIDST OF REJECTION

When witnessing to a Jewish person, you should expect to sometimes be met with anger and rejection, but you cannot allow that to stop you. You must be obedient in the midst of rejection. Yeshua brought God's message of love, hope, and salvation to Israel, even though He and His message were rejected. Many Jewish people will be like Jacob, who wrestled with Yahweh and afterwards was given a new name, walking with Him in a brand new way.

Even though Jewish people may become angry when you witness to them, oftentimes, their anger is the first step in their coming to faith. Yeshua was put on the cross, because people were angry with Him, but some of those, who were angry with Him, like Shaul, ended up coming to faith.

Just as Yeshua was crucified outside the city gates, a place of reproach and shame, you also have been called to suffer rejection for your faith.

> [8]*So do not be ashamed to testify about our Lord, or ashamed of me his prisoner. But join with me in suffering for the Gospel, by the power of God, ~2 Timothy 1:8 NIV*

Yeshua told us that if we are ashamed of Him, He will be ashamed of us when He comes again in the glory of the Father with the holy angels.

> [26]*"If anyone is ashamed of me and my words, the Son of Man will be ashamed of him when he comes in his glory and in the glory of the Father and of the holy angels." ~Luke 9:26 NIV*

Make obedience to Yeshua your primary goal. If you have Him in your heart, and He is real to you, then you have something to give, and God wants to use you to draw Jewish people to Himself. How can they believe, if they haven't heard?

> [14]*How, then, can they call on the one they have not believed in? And how can they believe in the one of*

> *whom they have not heard? And how can they hear*
> *without someone preaching to them? ~Romans 10:14*
> *NIV*

Many Christians say they love God, yet they never share their faith with anyone, because they're afraid they'll be rejected. Something is wrong when the only time a Christian will witness is when they're in an environment where everyone accepts them. *You need to make up your mind. Are you going to obey God, or are you going to be more concerned about what others think of you?*

When I was in Bible college, I went on a mission project with a Christian group; supposedly, to witness to Jewish people. To my amazement, when we arrived to do our witnessing, this group of Christians I was with never said anything about Jesus or His message. In fact, the traditional Jews, they were sent to, taught them about Orthodox Judaism. These "Christian missionaries" were more concerned about having the Jews like and accept them than they were about loving and obeying God.

If you're going to be an effective witness, you must be more concerned about loving and obeying God than you are with having people like and accept you. If you are going to reign with Him in glory, then you must be willing to suffer with Him.

> [17]*Now if we are children, then we are heirs—heirs of*
> *God and co-heirs with (Messiah), if indeed we share*
> *in his sufferings in order that we may also share in his*
> *glory. ~Romans 8:17 NIV*

The English word *martyr* is a direct translation of the Greek word for *witness*; so, if you are faithful and obedient in witnessing, you must expect to face rejection and martyrdom. Know that when you are rejected for your faith, you will become more convinced than ever that you are His. What a blessing that is!

> ¹⁶*"You did not choose me, but I chose you...*¹⁸*If the world hates you, keep in mind that it hated me first.* ¹⁹*If you belonged to the world, it would love you as its own. As it is, you do not belong to the world, but I have chosen you out of the world. That is why the world hates you." ~John 15:16a, 18-19 NIV*

> ¹⁰*"Blessed are those who are persecuted because of righteousness, for theirs is the kingdom of heaven.* ¹¹*Blessed are you when people insult you, persecute you and falsely say all kinds of evil against you because of me.* ¹²*Rejoice and be glad, because great is your reward in heaven, for in the same way they persecuted the prophets who were before you." ~Matthew 5:10-12 NIV*

It is a blessing, privilege, and honor to suffer because of our witness for Messiah.

2. BEING CONVINCED THAT JEWISH PEOPLE NEED YESHUA

Yahweh chose the Jewish people, out of all the peoples of the earth, to bring forth His plan of salvation for all people.

> ⁶*For you are a people holy to the LORD your God. The LORD your God has chosen you out of all the peoples on the face of the earth to be his people, his treasured possession. ~Deuteronomy 7:6 NIV*

Because the Jewish people are Yahweh's chosen ones, many Christians aren't convinced that Jewish people need

Yeshua for their salvation. When Yahweh says the Jewish people are His chosen people, it doesn't mean that every Jew is walking in relationship and fellowship with Him. Even though Jacob and Esau were both physical descendants of Abraham, Jacob was chosen, and Esau was not.

> ¹⁰*Not only that, but Rebekah's children had one and the same father, our father Isaac.* ¹¹*Yet, before the twins were born or had done anything good or bad—in order that God's purpose in election might stand:* ¹²*not by works but by him who calls—she was told, "The older will serve the younger."* ¹³*Just as it is written: "Jacob I loved, but Esau I hated." ~Romans 9:10-13 NIV*

> ⁹*For not all who are descended from Israel are Israel. ~Romans 9:6b NIV*

> ²⁷*Isaiah cries out concerning Israel: "Though the number of the Israelites be like the sand by the sea, only the remnant will be saved." ~Romans 9:27 NIV*

From these examples, you can now see that just because a person is Jewish, it doesn't necessarily mean they are walking in relationship with God. Even though the Jewish people are Yahweh's chosen ones, they must receive Yeshua as their Messiah, or they will die in their sins.

> ²⁴*"I told you that you would die in your sins; if you do not believe that I am the one I claim to be, you will indeed die in your sins." ~John 8:24 NIV*

Yeshua told the Jewish people that the only way they could have a true relationship with God was through Him. It was to the Jewish people that Yeshua said:

⁶"I am the way and the truth and the life. No one comes to the Father except through me." -John 14:6b NIV

I once heard someone say that modern-day Judaism, without its fulfillment in Yeshua, is like a man who intended to fly from Miami, Florida, to Los Angeles, California, but missed his connecting flight in New York City, and as a result, never reached his final destination. And so, too, the Law of Moses and the Prophets, without Yeshua, will not take one into heaven. It is critical for you to understand that modern-day Judaism, without its fulfillment in Yeshua, is insufficient to save.

3. BEING SENSITIVE TO PERSECUTION

When witnessing to Jewish people, be sensitive to the persecution they have experienced throughout history. Also, be aware of anti-Semitism they personally may have faced. You may even be led to apologize to them for the persecution done to the Jewish people in Yeshua's name. Explain to them that Yeshua is a Jew, who came for the Jews, and help them to understand His love for them.

²⁴But He answered and said, "I was sent only to the lost sheep of the house of Israel." -Matthew 15:24 NASB

¹¹He came to His own, and those who were His own did not receive Him. ¹²But as many as received Him, to them He gave the right to become children of God, even to those who believe in His name, -John 1:11-12 NASB

4. SHARING MESSIANIC PROPHECIES

Even though many Jewish people are secular and unfamiliar with Messianic prophecies, it will impact them when you show them in their own Hebrew Bible (Tanach –Old Testament) how Yeshua has fulfilled these prophecies. Familiarize yourself with the Messianic prophecies contained in chapter four of this book.

> [15] *Be diligent to present yourself approved to God, a worker who does not need to be ashamed, rightly dividing the word of truth. -2 Timothy 2:15 NKJV*

You must realize, though, that you may need to build a Jewish person's faith in the scriptures for them to be impressed by the Messianic prophecies. Be aware that many Jewish people do not believe that their Hebrew Bible is the revealed Word of God. Instead, they believe that the Bible is man's evolving concept of who they think God is. In other words, many Jews think that the Bible's origins lie in man rather than God. It will be imperative for you to share with them how they can trust the authenticity of the Bible.

A. AUTHENTICITY OF THE BIBLE – INTELLIGENCE WITHIN CREATION

One of the ways you can demonstrate the authenticity of the Bible to a Jewish person is by showing them the intelligence that is built into creation. Ask them, "Do you believe that God created the world and mankind? Do you believe the first verse of the Torah that says, 'In the beginning God created the heavens and the earth.'?"

If the Jewish person doesn't believe that God created the universe, explain to them how the theory of evolution isn't possible, because it doesn't account for the intelligent design that is built into creation. The fact that there is intelligence within creation can only be explained by the fact that it was designed by an Intelligent Creator (God). Evolutionists cannot logically explain the built-in intelligence within creation. Intelligence within creation can only be explained by coming to grips with the fact that an Intelligent Designer (God) fashioned it.

Illustrate to them how our own bodies point to an Intelligent Designer. Explain how our bodies have an automatic cooling system (sweating) to keep us from overheating and how our bodies automatically produce antibodies to fight off disease and infection when we get sick. These bodily processes are not random; rather, they have been built into us by an Intelligent Creator.

Describe all the ways in which our universe testifies to being created by an Intelligent Designer. Illustrate how the sun is the precise distance from the earth in order to sustain life. If the earth was any closer to the sun, we would burn up; if it was any farther away, we would freeze to death. Explain to them how the birds instinctively know to fly south in the winter and north in the summer.

To believe that our universe is just the result of evolution, instead of the design of an Intelligent Designer, is like believing that a bottle of spilled ink landing on a piece of paper would produce a perfect picture of a house with a fence around it, with mom, dad, and the dog standing at the front door. The only way to have a picture with that kind of detail is for someone with intelligence to paint it, and so it is with the universe.

Explain to them that morality cannot exist, if the theory of evolution is true. Morality, also, cannot exist, if we are just the result of some cosmic explosion in space or the result of something that bubbled up from a chemical reaction; but the reality is that morality does exist.

Take, for example, an individual that argues that there is no absolute standard of right and wrong, but rather that morality is culturally defined. You will find, however, that if someone kills their child or rapes their wife, they are outraged, and they want justice now.

But if morality is defined by the individual or culture, there can be no justice, and murder and rape are not necessarily wrong. This one, who formally claimed there was no absolute standard of right and wrong, suddenly realizes, after he's been violated, that there is absolute morality. This one that had been arguing that there is no absolute standard, and that morality is defined by the individual or culture, comes to realize that murder and rape violate a moral code that has been written into the heart of humanity.

Another example of this is the individual who argues that there is no absolute right or wrong, who then has something stolen from him. When he has something stolen from him, he shouts out, "That's not right. He stole that from me." This cry of injustice comes from deep within his being. Suddenly, he knows the difference between right and wrong. The reality is, beloved, that morality does exit.

People groups from all over the world somehow know the difference between right and wrong. Only God, the moral lawgiver, could have placed that knowledge of right and wrong within all mankind. If there is no God, there could be no absolute right or wrong, but there is, and when push comes to shove, all people know it.

B. AUTHENTICITY OF
THE BIBLE – ARCHAEOLOGY

Another way of demonstrating the authenticity of the Bible is through the field of archaeology. For years, some have questioned the existence of certain people mentioned in the Bible, but recently in Israel, archaeology has uncovered proof that these people truly did exist. One example of this is the biblical ruler, Pontius Pilate (Matthew 27:11-26). For years there was no historical record of his life, and archeologists perceived the biblical description of his life to be purely fictitious. A few years ago, however, several stones were uncovered in Israel that had the name of Pontius Pilate engraved upon them. Due to archaeological discoveries like this, we see that the Bible is historically accurate and can be trusted.

C. AUTHENTICITY OF THE BIBLE –
ISRAEL'S EXISTENCE TODAY

The amazing reality of the supernatural survival of the nation of Israel throughout history is another way to demonstrate the authenticity of the Bible. The Torah, the Prophets, and the New Testament all teach that God will preserve Israel. Explain to the Jewish person how so many powerful empires have come and gone throughout history. The Roman Empire has come and gone, the Persian Empire has come and gone, and the Babylonian Empire has come and gone; yet, today, the Jewish people still exist and flourish in the small nation of Israel. They exist today, having survived the Crusades and the Nazi holocaust, because they are Yahweh's chosen covenant people. He supernaturally protects the nation of Israel in the midst of their enemies, who totally surround them.

The Jewish people are under Yahweh's divine protection, because they have a specific role to play. According to scripture, they are the Chosen Ones who brought the revelation of monotheism to the world. Through them, Yahweh brought the Messiah into the world, and one day He will use them to call Messiah back. The survival of Israel is of utter importance, since all future prophecies concerning end times are connected to them and their salvation. The fact that their God, Yahweh, has preserved them as a people for over 3500 years, while other people groups have disappeared, testifies to the authenticity and trustworthiness of the Bible.

5. SHARING YOUR PERSONAL TESTIMONY

Another witnessing strategy to Jewish people is to simply share with them your personal testimony. By sharing your personal experiences of what Yeshua has done in your life, you will help others realize how real He is. Explain how He has answered your prayers. Share how you have a love relationship with Him and how, through Him, you have intimacy with God. Sharing your experiences is a great witnessing tool, because it is difficult to dispute someone's personal testimony.

6. ALLOWING THE HOLY SPIRIT TO GUIDE YOU

When witnessing, be sensitive to the Holy Spirit's inner witness in your heart, and trust in His anointing to lead you. Allow Him to be your guide in knowing what to say and what not to say. Pay attention as to whether you feel His peace to continue witnessing, or whether He's giving you a check to stop. Sometimes, once you've spoken, silence can be the Holy Spirit's most effective way of making impact.

7. DON'T BECOME INTIMIDATED

When witnessing to a Jewish person, guard yourself against being intimidated. Jewish people may make Gentiles feel as if they are being looked down upon. Being Jewish, I believe this phenomenon takes place for at least three reasons. First of all, because Jewish people are a minority and have been discriminated against, they have developed a defensive technique that can cause Gentiles and outsiders to feel as if they are being treated in a condescending way. Second of all, some Jewish people feel they are superior, because the Torah says they are God's chosen people. Thirdly, Jewish people sometimes perceive the Gentile's Christian faith as being inferior to theirs.

Because we, as followers of Messiah Yeshua, believe in the mystery of the Godhead (Father, Son, and Holy Spirit), some Jews view our faith as pagan and polytheistic. Of course, we believe there is only one God, but Jewish people, sometimes, accuse us of believing in three Gods. The bottom line is that you cannot allow the way they perceive you to intimidate you or affect the way you see yourself.

The Israelites allowed themselves to become intimidated by their enemy, when they began to view themselves through their enemy's eyes. This weakness cost them entrance into the Promised Land. This happened when the children of Israel went to spy out the Promised Land (Numbers 13). They became so intimidated by the Nephilim, who were living there, that they began to see themselves through their enemy's eyes as small and weak.

²⁶They came back to Moses and Aaron and the whole Israelite community at Kadesh in the Desert of Paran. There they reported to them and to the whole assembly and showed them the fruit of the land. ²⁷They gave Moses this account: "We went into the land to which you sent us, and it does flow with milk and honey! Here is its fruit. ²⁸But the people who live there are powerful, and the cities are fortified and very large. We even saw descendants of Anak there. ²⁹Amalekites live in the Negev; the Hittites, Jebusites and Amorites live in the hill country; and the Canaanites live near the sea and along the Jordan." ³⁰Then Caleb silenced the people before Moses and said, "We should go up and take possession of the land, for we can certainly do it." ³¹But the men who had gone up with him said, "We can't attack those people; they are stronger than we are." ³²And they spread among the Israelites a bad report about the land they had explored. They said, "The land we explored devours those living in it. All the people we saw there are of great size. ³³We saw the Nephilim there (the descendants of Anak come from the Nephilim). <u>We seemed like grasshoppers in our own eyes, and we looked the same to them.</u>*" (emphasis added) -Numbers 13:26-33 NIV*

When witnessing, don't allow yourself to be intimidated. Don't allow others to cause you to see yourself through their eyes. Instead, maintain your boldness. Yeshua HaMashiach is the Way, the Truth, and the Life, and you have been commanded to be His witness. So don't be intimidated if you run into a Jewish person who may treat you condescendingly. The Jews are God's chosen people in the sense that revelation came to the world through them, but you are God's chosen ambassador to proclaim to them that Yeshua is their Messiah!

8. REMEMBER – YOU ARE THE KEY

You have come into a relationship with the God of Abraham, Isaac, and Jacob, for the purpose of provoking God's ancient covenant people to jealousy.

> [11]*Again I ask: Did they stumble so as to fall beyond recovery? Not at all! Rather, because of their transgression, <u>salvation has come to the Gentiles to make Israel envious.</u> (emphasis added) ~Romans 11:11 NIV*

Remember, you are the key for that Jewish person to hear about Yeshua. If you don't share Yeshua with them, who will?

> [13]*for, "Everyone who calls on the name of the Lord will be saved." [14]How, then, can they call on the one they have not believed in? And how can they believe in the one of whom they have not heard? And how can they hear without someone preaching to them? ~Romans 10:13-14 NIV*

9. LEND THEM A BIBLE

Encourage your Jewish friend to read the Bible. If they don't have one, don't give them one of yours, and don't buy them one. Instead, lend them one of yours, and tell them you need it back in a couple of weeks. By lending them your Bible, rather than giving them one or buying them one, you create a sense of urgency for them to read it. Encourage them to read about God's love for Israel in Romans, chapters 9, 10, and 11. Check back on them, in a week or so, to make sure they've understood what they've read. This strategy of lending your Bible is one which will work for both Jew and Gentile.

10. AVOID USING CHRISTIAN JARGON

When witnessing to Jewish people, use terms they will understand. Avoid using Christian jargon such as Trinity, redeemed, or washed by the blood of the Lamb. These terms may have deep meaning for a believer, but they probably won't have any meaning to the Jewish person you're trying to reach with the message of Messiah. In fact, these terms could, instead, isolate the Jewish person and decrease their reception of your witness. If you do happen to use a term they don't understand, be sure to explain it.

11. MEETING PEOPLE WHERE THEY ARE

In Acts 17, we read how the apostle Paul (Shaul) witnessed to the Gentiles on Mars Hill in Athens, Greece. He didn't start by telling them about the Torah; because, as Gentiles, they wouldn't have known anything about the Torah. Instead, he met them where they were and used it as a bridge to bring them to the truth. He appealed to them about their worship of many gods, one of them being an unknown God. Shaul explained that this unknown God, they were worshipping, was the One true and living God. By meeting them where they were, Shaul could then bring them to the knowledge of the truth.

So whether you are witnessing to Jew or Gentile, follow Shaul's example of meeting people where they are. Even Yeshua, Himself, took on flesh and blood and became one of us, in order to reach us. So when sharing your faith with a Jewish person, do your best to share with them in a way they can identify with. By doing this, you will be in a stronger position to bring them to an understanding of the message of Yeshua Messiah.

One way you could do this is by helping a Jewish person understand how Yeshua fulfills their holidays given to them in the Torah. For example, you could point out how they set an empty seat for Elijah (Eliyahu) at Passover. The reason they do this is because their Bible teaches them that Elijah will come before Messiah (Malachi 4:5). After pointing this out, you could then share with them that Yeshua said that John the Baptist was Elijah (Matthew 11:14) and that Yeshua, Himself, was the One whom Elijah said was to come.

> [14]*"And if you are willing to accept it, he is the Elijah who was to come." -Matthew 11:14 NIV*

You can use the New Testament as a bridge to reach Jewish people by showing them how the very first verse, Matthew 1:1, connects Yeshua to the Torah in the Hebrew Bible.

> [1]*This is a record of the ancestors of Jesus the Messiah, a descendant of David and of Abraham: -Matthew 1:1 NLT*

CONQUERING THEOLOGICAL OBJECTIONS

I often receive feedback from Jewish people in response to my proclaiming Yeshua as Messiah. As you can probably imagine, most of the feedback I receive is antagonistic. Jewish people often tell me that "Jews believe this" or "Jews don't believe that" as a justification for their rejection of Yeshua as Messiah.

What is important for a Jew to realize is that the truth isn't necessarily defined by what the rabbis believe, individual belief, or even what the majority believe. It wasn't that long ago that the majority of people believed that the earth was flat, but that didn't make it true. It was even more recently that Nazi Germany and their allies believed that the world's problems could be solved by the elimination of the Jewish people. The point is: truth isn't defined by what people believe. God is truth, and the benchmark of truth is God's Word.

In this next section, I will share several theological objections Jewish people may have in accepting Yeshua as their Messiah. In responding to these objections, I hope to better equip you to help them to receive the truth of God's Word.

1. CHRISTIAN DOCTRINE OF THE TRINITY

One theological objection Jewish people have in their acceptance of Yeshua revolves around the Christian doctrine of the *trinity*. The word *trinity* is not found in the Bible. It is a term which was coined by the early church fathers to explain God manifesting Himself in three ways: the Father, Son, and Holy Spirit. When Christians mention the *trinity*, Jewish people have the misconception that Christians are worshipping three separate gods. They don't understand that Christians are worshipping just one multidimensional God, who manifests Himself in three different ways: the Father, Son, and Holy Spirit.

The most famous declaration in Judaism is the Sh'ma.

⁴Hear, O Israel: The LORD our God, the LORD is one. ~Deuteronomy 6:4 NIV

In Hebrew:

⁴Sh'ma Israel, Adonai Eloheinu, Adonai echad. ~D'Varim 6:4

In the Sh'ma, the Hebrew word *echad* is translated as *one*. This is why it is difficult for a Jewish person to understand God manifesting Himself in three ways. Although *echad* is often translated as *one*, it doesn't necessarily imply a singular unity.

In the Sh'ma, God was not asserting that He couldn't manifest Himself in more than one way; rather, He was affirming that He <u>alone</u> was God. At the time the Torah was given to the Israelites, most people on earth were worshipping many gods. As a result, God was simply declaring that He <u>only</u> was God. The Stone Edition of the Chumash Artscroll Series (a traditional Jewish Bible) translates Deuteronomy 6:4 this way: "Here, O Israel: HASHEM is our God, HASHEM is the One and Only." (HASHEM, which in Hebrew literally means "The Name," is the Jewish way of referring to the name of God.) I believe that when the LORD declared that He was *echad* in Deuteronomy 6:4, He was not seeking to reveal the inner mysteries of His essence or nature, but He was declaring to a pagan culture that He, Yahweh, was the One True God.

Furthermore, in the Torah, the word *echad* can also refer to a compound unity. One example of this is in Genesis 2:24, where scripture describes how a man leaves his mother and father to be joined to his wife, and the two become *echad* (one).

> [24]*For this reason a man will leave his father and mother and be united to his wife, and they will become one flesh. ~Genesis 2:24 NIV*

Another example in scripture where the word *echad* refers to a compound unity is when the Israelites combined individual pieces of the Tabernacle together, and they became *echad* (one).

Jewish people need to recognize that God can reveal Himself as Father, Son, and Holy Spirit, all at the same time, and still be *one* God. For example, at creation, God refers to Himself in the plural forms of *us* and *our*.

> [26]*Then God said, "Let <u>us</u> make man in our image, in <u>our</u> likeness," (emphasis added)* ~Genesis 1:26a NIV

In fact, God's name first appears in the Hebrew Bible in Genesis 1:1 as *Elohim*. *Elohim* is a Hebrew name for God denoting plurality. In choosing to first manifest Himself to us as *Elohim*, God is revealing His multidimensional nature. The fact that *Elohim* is a plural, rather than a singular name for God, suggests, once again, that He is multidimensional, rather than a singular unity.

In the B'rit Chadashah (New Testament), when Yeshua was being immersed in the Jordan River, Elohim revealed His multidimensional nature when He disclosed Himself as Father, Son, and Holy Spirit, all at the same time. The Father spoke from heaven while the Son (Yeshua) was being immersed, and at the same time, the Ruach HaKodesh (the Holy Spirit) appeared as a dove above Yeshua's head.

> [16]*As soon as Jesus was baptized, he went up out of the water. At that moment heaven was opened, and he saw the Spirit of God descending like a dove and lighting on him.* [17]*And a voice from heaven said, "This is my Son, whom I love; with him I am well pleased."* ~Matthew 3:16-17 NIV

This concept of the plurality of God's nature is understood by many Jews who have studied the Kabbalah. The word Kabbalah means "to receive" or "receiving." According to Wikipedia, Kabbalah is a discipline and school of thought concerned with the mystical aspect of Judaism. Although

I personally do not endorse the Kabbalah, I appreciate its mystical approach in seeking to comprehend the plurality of God's nature. My point in bringing up the Kabbalah is to help both Jews and Gentiles to understand that the concept of the plurality of God's nature is not as foreign to Jewish thought as many have been led to believe.

It is imperative for you to help Jewish people understand that the doctrine of the *trinity* is not anti-Jewish, foreign to mystical Jewish thought, or outside the parameters of the Torah. Although I do not like the word *trinity,* because it feels so anti-Jewish to me because of my Jewish culture, I do believe that God is multidimensional and that He has revealed Himself as Father, Son, and Holy Spirit. The LORD desires to use you to help Jewish people understand that although He has revealed Himself in the B'rit Chadashah (New Testament) as Father, Son, and Holy Spirit, He is still <u>One</u> God, and He <u>alone</u> is God as stated in the Sh'ma.

2. YESHUA – GOD IN THE FLESH

Another theological objection Jewish people have in acknowledging Yeshua as Messiah is the concept of Him being God in the flesh. This is a difficult concept for most Jewish people, because they believe God cannot become human. The New Testament concept of God in the flesh does not diminish who God is. Christians aren't saying that God is simply a man, but rather that He took upon human flesh to become one with us.

> [1]*In the beginning was the Word, and the Word was with God, and the Word was God.* [14]*The Word became flesh and made his dwelling among us.* ~John 1:1,14a NIV

Jewish people have the misconception that Christians are worshipping a man when they see pictures or statues of Yeshua. Christians are not worshipping a man, but rather God, who became man in order to redeem us. He did this because of His great love for mankind, whom He created in His own image. The only way He could reach us and save us was to become one of us. Christians are not worshipping a man but rather God in human flesh.

Although Yeshua was fully man, He also proclaimed to be God. He stated that He and God the Father were one.

> [30]*"I and the Father are one." ~John 10:30 NIV*

> [22]*"I have given them the glory that you gave me, that they may be one as we are one:" ~John 17:22 NIV*

In the Torah, in Genesis 18, Yahweh appeared to Abraham (Avraham) in human form.

> [1]*The LORD appeared to Abraham near the great trees of Mamre while he was sitting at the entrance to his tent in the heat of the day. [2]Abraham looked up and saw three men standing nearby. When he saw them, he hurried from the entrance of his tent to meet them and bowed low to the ground. ~Genesis 18:1-2 NIV*

Abraham actually saw and spoke to Yahweh and prepared a meal in which the two of them ate together.

> [7]*Then he ran to the herd and selected a choice, tender calf and gave it to a servant, who hurried to prepare it. [8]He then brought some curds and milk and the calf that had been prepared, and set these before them. While they ate, he stood near them under a tree. ~Genesis 18:7-8 NIV*

The reason we know that Abraham actually saw and ate with God in human form is because the Hebrew text actually says that the man that Abraham saw and ate with was the LORD (Yahweh). Just as Yahweh took upon a human body to eat a meal with Abraham, so likewise did Yeshua after His resurrection.

> [36]*While they were still talking about this, Jesus himself stood among them and said to them, "Peace be with you."*... [39]*"Look at my hands and my feet. It is I myself! Touch me and see; a ghost does not have flesh and bones, as you see I have."* [40]*When he had said this, he showed them his hands and feet.* [41]*And while they still did not believe it because of joy and amazement, he asked them, "Do you have anything here to eat?"* [42]*They gave him a piece of broiled fish,* [43]*and he took it and ate it in their presence.* ~Luke 24:36, 39-43 NIV

Yahweh came to earth in human flesh as Yeshua because of His great love for us. In this love, He died on the cross, becoming the sacrifice for all mankind's sin. When we receive Yeshua Messiah through faith, we then enter into a relationship with Yahweh, the God of the universe.

3. YESHUA – THE SON OF GOD

Another theological objection Jewish people have in acknowledging Yeshua as Messiah is the concept that Yeshua is the Son of God. A study of the Hebrew scriptures, however, clearly reveals the concept of sonship with God.

Yahweh called Israel His son.

> [22]*"...Then say to Pharaoh, 'This is what the LORD says: Israel is my firstborn son,* [23]*and I told you, "Let*

123

my son go, so he may worship me." But you refused to let him go; so I will kill your firstborn son.'" ~Exodus 4:22-23 NIV

Yahweh referred to King David as His son.

[14]"I will be his father, and he will be my son. When he does wrong, I will punish him with the rod of men, with floggings inflicted by men." ~2 Samuel 7:14 NIV

If Yahweh called Israel His son, and referred to King David as His son, doesn't it make sense that He would call the Messiah His Son. This is clearly revealed in Psalm 2, which is widely acknowledged as a psalm about the Messiah.

[7]I will proclaim the decree of the LORD: He said to me, "You are my Son; today I have become your Father." ~Psalm 2:7 NIV

My favorite illustration in the Hebrew Bible revealing Messiah as God's Son is found in the book of Daniel. Daniel (Dani'el), one of Judaism's great prophets, writes of a powerful vision he has of the "son" in the last days.

[13]"In my vision at night I looked, and there before me was one like a <u>son of man</u>, coming with the clouds of heaven. He approached the Ancient of Days and was led into his presence. [14]He was given authority, glory and sovereign power; all peoples, nations and men of every language worshiped him. His dominion is an everlasting dominion that will not pass away, and his kingdom is one that will never be destroyed." (emphasis added) ~Daniel 7:13-14 NIV

Who is this "son of man" that Daniel speaks of? This son is Yeshua, who is both the son of man (speaking of His humanity) and the son of God (speaking of His divinity.

> [67]*"If You are the (Messiah), tell us." But He said to them, "If I tell you, you will not believe;* [68]*and if I ask a question, you will not answer.* [69]*But from now on THE SON OF MAN WILL BE SEATED AT THE RIGHT HAND of the power OF GOD."* [70]*And they all said, "Are You the Son of God, then?" And He said to them, "Yes, I am." (emphasis added) ~Luke 22:67-70 NASB*

The prophet Isaiah (Yesha`yahu), likewise, reveals the mystery of the person of God's son. He calls Him: Wonderful Counselor, Mighty God, Everlasting Father, and the Prince of Peace.

> [6]*For to us a child is born, to us a son is given, and the government will be on His shoulders. And He will be called Wonderful Counselor, Mighty God, Everlasting Father, Prince of Peace.* [7]*Of the increase of his government and peace there will be no end. He will reign on David's throne and over his kingdom, establishing and upholding it with justice and righteousness from that time on and forever. The zeal of the LORD Almighty will accomplish this. (emphasis added) ~Isaiah 9:6-7 NIV*

This scripture straightforwardly reveals Messiah as both God's Son (for to us a child is born, to us a son is given) and as God Himself (and He will be called ... Mighty God).

Family units on earth, consisting of moms, dads, sons, and daughters, are a reflection of the mystery that there is family relationship within God Himself. I am not suggesting that there is more than one God but rather that there is relationship within God.

> ²⁶*Then God said, "Let <u>Us</u> make man in <u>Our</u> image, according to <u>Our</u> likeness;" (emphasis added) ~Genesis 1:26a NASB*

From the very beginning of the Torah, you discover that there is relationship within God Himself, and Yeshua is a reflection of that intimacy.

> ¹⁸*No one has seen God at any time; the only begotten God <u>who is in the bosom of the Father</u>, He has explained Him. (emphasis added) ~John 1:18 NASB*

Our sons and daughters on earth are a physical manifestation of the relationship that has always existed in God Himself. Scripture reveals that God does have a Son, His name is Yeshua, and He has always been in the bosom of the Father.

---

4. I DON'T NEED TO BE SAVED – I'M A JEW

Many Jewish people believe that they have no need for salvation, because they already are God's chosen people. On that basis, they falsely believe they automatically go to heaven. Jewish people's pride in their ethnicity has become a roadblock to their salvation. Many Jews of Yeshua's day were not able to receive Him for this exact reason.

> ³⁶*"So if the Son sets you free, you will be free indeed. ³⁷I know you are Abraham's descendants. Yet you are ready to kill me, because you have no room for my word. ³⁸I am telling you what I have seen in the Father's presence, and you do what you have heard from your father." ³⁹"Abraham is our father," they answered. "If you were Abraham's children," said Jesus, "then you would do the things Abraham did. ⁴⁰As it is, you are determined*

to kill me, a man who has told you the truth that I heard from God. Abraham did not do such things. ⁴¹You are doing the things your own father does." "We are not illegitimate children," they protested. "The only Father we have is God himself." ⁴²Jesus said to them, "If God were your Father, you would love me, for I came from God and now am here. I have not come on my own; but he sent me. ⁴³Why is my language not clear to you? Because you are unable to hear what I say." ~John 8:36-43 NIV

⁵⁶*"Your father Abraham rejoiced at the thought of seeing my day; he saw it and was glad." ⁵⁷"You are not yet fifty years old," the Jews said to him, "and you have seen Abraham!" ⁵⁸"I tell you the truth," Jesus answered, "before Abraham was born, I am!" ⁵⁹At this, they picked up stones to stone him, but Jesus hid himself, slipping away from the temple grounds. ~John 8:56-59 NIV*

The Jews of Yeshua's day took pride in the fact that they were Abraham's physical descendants. They thought they had a place in the world to come just by the nature of the fact that they were born Jews. Yeshua, however, said to them:

²⁴*"unless you believe that I am He, you will die in your sins." ~John 8:24b NASB*

Similarly, Jewish people today take security in being Jewish. A careful study of scripture, however, reveals that this whole concept is erroneous. Consider Moses' words to the Israelites of his day as recorded in the Torah.

²⁷*"For I know how rebellious and stiff-necked you are. If you have been rebellious against the LORD while I*

*am still alive and with you, how much more will you
rebel after I die!* [28] *Assemble before me all the elders of
your tribes and all your officials, so that I can speak
these words in their hearing and call heaven and earth
to testify against them.* [29] *For I know that after my
death you are sure to become utterly corrupt and to
turn from the way I have commanded you. In days
to come, disaster will fall upon you because you will
do evil in the sight of the LORD and provoke him to
anger by what your hands have made."* -Deuteronomy
31:27-29 NIV

These verses, as well as other writings in the Torah, reveal
that the majority of the nation of Israel was not walking in
the favor of God or in His blessing, and it is the same way
today. Jewish people must receive salvation; their heritage
of being born Jewish will not save them. This salvation
only comes through Messiah Yeshua. The literal meaning
of Yeshua in Hebrew is salvation, and He is the only One
by which one may be saved.

5. I HAVE NO NEED FOR
A SAVIOR – I'M A GOOD PERSON

Another theological objection some Jewish people
have in acknowledging Yeshua as Messiah is the concept
of believing they are secure in their salvation by the virtue
of their own good works. Many fail to see that only God
is righteous, and mankind falls woefully short. In other
words, a Jewish person may believe they have no need for
Yeshua to be their Savior, since they already believe they are
a good person. Many times, we tend to measure ourselves by
comparing ourselves to each other, rather than comparing
ourselves to God's holiness.

¹²*but when they measure themselves by themselves and compare themselves with themselves, they are without understanding.* ~2 *Corinthians 10:12b NASB*

Israel's great prophet, Isaiah, found that when he stood before the LORD, he couldn't compare himself to others but had to see himself in the light of God's presence and holiness.

¹*In the year of King Uzziah's death I saw the LORD sitting on a throne, lofty and exalted, with the train of His robe filling the temple.* ²*Seraphim stood above Him, each having six wings: with two he covered his face, and with two he covered his feet, and with two he flew.* ³*And one called out to another and said, "Holy Holy, Holy, is the LORD of hosts, The whole earth is full of His glory."* ⁴*And the foundations of the thresholds trembled at the voice of him who called out, while the temple was filling with smoke.* ⁵*Then I said, "Woe is me, for I am ruined! Because I am a man of unclean lips, And I live among a people of unclean lips; For my eyes have seen the King, the LORD of hosts."* ~*Isaiah 6:1-5 NASB*

The Pharisees of Yeshua's day sought to establish their own righteousness through their good works, instead of allowing God, in His grace, to impart His righteousness to them.

³*For not knowing about God's righteousness and seeking to establish their own, they did not subject themselves to the righteousness of God.* ~*Romans 10:3 NASB*

The apostle Paul (Shaul) stated that if righteousness could be obtained through our own good works, then there would be no need for the grace of God, and Yeshua died for nothing.

> [21]*"I do not nullify the grace of God, for if righteousness comes through the Law, then (Messiah) died needlessly."*
> ~*Galatians 2:21 NASB*

In fact, the apostle Paul (Shaul) crystallized this whole argument in the book of Philippians.

> [4]*If anyone else has a mind to put confidence in the flesh, I far more:* [5]*circumcised the eighth day, of the nation of Israel, of the tribe of Benjamin, a Hebrew of Hebrews; as to the Law, a Pharisee;* [6]*as to zeal, a persecutor of the church; as to the righteousness which is in the Law, found blameless.* [7]*But whatever things were gain to me, those things I have counted as loss for the sake of (Messiah).* [8]*More than that, I count all things to be loss in view of the surpassing value of knowing (Messiah) Jesus my Lord, for whom I have suffered the loss of all things, and count them but rubbish so that I may gain (Messiah),* [9]*and may be found in Him, not having a righteousness of my own derived from the Law, but that which is through faith in (Messiah), the righteousness which comes from God on the basis of faith,* ~*Philippians 3:4b-9 NASB*

You must help the Jewish person understand that no matter how good they are, they will never be good enough to meet the perfect standards of God. They will never be able to obtain righteousness on their own. It is only God who can impart His righteousness to us, and this righteousness is imparted to us through our faith in Messiah Yeshua.

6. SUBSTITUTIONARY SACRIFICIAL ATONEMENT

Another theological objection Jewish people have in acknowledging Yeshua as Messiah is their acceptance of their need for a blood sacrifice for their sin. God's way of forgiving man's sin is through the principle of substitutionary sacrificial atonement, which is conveyed by blood. Substitutionary sacrificial atonement means that an innocent one (substitute) can die (sacrifice) in the place of the guilty to make atonement, thus releasing the guilty one from the penalty of death.

> [4]*"The soul who sins will die." -Ezekiel 18:4b NASB*

> [23]*For the wages of sin is death, -Romans 6:23a NIV*

> [11]*"For the life of a creature is in the blood, and I have given it to you to make atonement for yourselves on the altar; it is the blood that makes atonement for one's life." -Leviticus 17:11 NIV*

The penalty for sin against Yahweh is death, and an innocent one must die in the place of the guilty for atonement to be made. This death is symbolized by blood, since the life of the flesh is in the blood; it is for this reason, we have the blood atonements prescribed in scripture.

So, once again, the principle of "substitutionary sacrificial atonement," is defined as an innocent being dying in the place of the guilty. Since the life of the flesh is in the blood (Leviticus 17:11), the blood of the sacrifice must be poured out, thus symbolizing that its life has been given. In this exchange, the punishment of the guilty one is taken out on the innocent one, thus releasing the guilty one of his sin and granting him forgiveness.

Even though Jewish people today do not recognize their need for a blood sacrifice for their sin, the Torah is very clear that one is necessary. We are now going to examine this by looking at the Passover, the Covenant at Sinai, the daily sacrifices in the Tabernacle and Temple, and Yom Kippur (the Day of Atonement).

A. AN OVERVIEW OF
ATONEMENT AND BLOOD IN SCRIPTURE

a. THE PASSOVER

We see the concept of substitutionary sacrificial atonement first illustrated in the Torah at Passover, when the blood of an unblemished lamb was applied to the doorposts of the Israelites' homes, so the punishment of death would pass over them. (Exodus 12) The B'rit Chadashah (New Testament) reveals to us that Yeshua is the fulfillment of the ancient Passover lamb.

> [7]*For (Messiah), our Passover lamb, has been sacrificed.*
> *~1 Corinthians 5:7b NIV*

Yeshua chose to be crucified on Passover to demonstrate that He was the fulfillment of this Appointed Day of the LORD. (Leviticus 23:5)

Yeshua's ministry began with Him coming to the Jordan River to be immersed with the rest of Israel by John the Baptist. At this event, John pointed at Yeshua and declared to the Jews, who were assembled there, "Behold the Lamb of God." In doing this, John was identifying Yeshua as the fulfillment of the ancient Passover.

²⁹*The next day John saw Jesus coming toward him and said, "Look, the Lamb of God," ~John 1:29a NIV*

In fact, the last meal that Yeshua ate with His disciples was a Passover meal. At this Passover meal, Yeshua took the matzah (bread) and wine, blessed it, then gave it to His disciples and told them to eat and drink of it. Furthermore, He told His disciples that the matzah and the wine represented Him, and by partaking of it, they would symbolically be partaking of Him, even as the ancient Israelites were instructed to eat the Passover lamb 3,500 years ago. (Exodus 12)

¹*Now the Feast of Unleavened Bread, which is called the Passover, was approaching.* ²*The chief priests and the scribes were seeking how they might put Him to death; for they were afraid of the people.* ³*And Satan entered into Judas who was called Iscariot, belonging to the number of the twelve.* ⁴*And he went away and discussed with the chief priests and officers how he might betray Him to them.* ⁵*They were glad and agreed to give him money.* ⁶*So he consented, and began seeking a good opportunity to betray Him to them apart from the crowd.* ⁷*Then came the first day of Unleavened Bread on which the Passover lamb had to be sacrificed.* ⁸*And Jesus sent Peter and John, saying, "Go and prepare the Passover for us, so that we may eat it."* ⁹*They said to Him, "Where do You want us to prepare it?"* ¹⁰*And He said to them, "When you have entered the city, a man will meet you carrying a pitcher of water; follow him into the house that he enters.* ¹¹*"And you shall say to the owner of the house, 'The Teacher says to you, "Where is the guest room in which I may eat the Passover with My disciples?"'* ¹²*"And he will show you a large, furnished upper room; prepare it there."* ¹³*And they left*

and found everything just as He had told them; and they prepared the Passover.

[14]*When the hour had come, He reclined at the table, and the apostles with Him.* [15]*And He said to them, "I have earnestly desired to eat this Passover with you before I suffer;* [16]*for I say to you, I shall never again eat it until it is fulfilled in the kingdom of God."* [17]*And when He had taken a cup and given thanks, He said, "Take this and share it among yourselves;* [18]*for I say to you, I will not drink of the fruit of the vine from now on until the kingdom of God comes."* [19]*And when He had taken some bread and given thanks, He broke it and gave it to them, saying, "This is My body which is given for you; do this in remembrance of Me."* [20]*And in the same way He took the cup after they had eaten, saying, "This cup which is poured out for you is the new covenant in My blood." ~Luke 22:1-20 NASB*

b. THE COVENANT AT MT. SINAI

We have seen that God first used blood to deliver Israel out of Egypt, through the blood of the Passover lamb. Next, notice how the LORD used blood to seal the Covenant He made with them at Mt. Sinai.

[8]*Moses then took the blood, sprinkled it on the people and said, "This is the blood of the covenant that the LORD has made with you in accordance with all these words." ~Exodus 24:8 NIV*

Why did Yahweh sprinkle Israel with blood when they received His Covenant at Mt. Sinai? Yahweh did this, because an eternal Covenant between a holy God and sinful humanity can only exist through the blood of a substitutionary sacrificial atonement. The author of the book of Hebrews calls it "the blood of the eternal covenant." (Hebrews 13:20)

c. THE TABERNACLE/TEMPLE

After Yahweh gave Israel the Covenant at Mt. Sinai and sprinkled them with blood, He then gave them specific instructions for the building of the Tabernacle. (Exodus 25) The Tabernacle was to be constructed, so Yahweh could dwell among and have fellowship with the nation of Israel. If an Israelite worshipper desired to meet with Yahweh, he had to come to the Tabernacle and bring with him a blood sacrifice. (Leviticus 1:1-5)

When the worshipper brought his blood sacrifice (unblemished animal) to the Tabernacle, the priest would bind it on the altar. The worshipper would then place his hands on the head of his sacrifice, thus transferring his sin into the sacrifice. The animal was then put to death, through the shedding of blood, symbolizing, once again, that an innocent one had died in the place of a guilty one, thus releasing the guilty one of his sin. The worshipper could now have fellowship with Yahweh, because his sin had been transferred into the sacrifice that had been put to death in his place, symbolized through the shedding of blood.

I hope you can see that the Torah reveals that a blood sacrifice is necessary in order for humankind to be in relationship with God. We see this climaxed in the highest Jewish holiday of the year, Yom Kippur (the Day of Atonement).

d. YOM KIPPUR (THE DAY OF ATONEMENT)

Yom Kippur is Hebrew for "the Day of Atonement" or "the Day of Covering." For the traditional Jewish community, Yom Kippur is the most holy day on the Jewish calendar. It was on this day that Yahweh forgave the sins of His people, Israel, each year.

Within the Tabernacle and Temple there was both a Holy Place and a Holy of Holies. The High Priest could enter the Holy Place everyday, but he could only enter the Holy of Holies one day a year on Yom Kippur. On Yom Kippur, the High Priest would enter the Holy of Holies with the blood of a bull for his own sin, and the blood of a goat for the sin of Israel. This blood was poured upon the altar on the Ark of the Covenant. When Yahweh saw the blood poured out upon the altar, He covered the sins of His people, Israel. This is why Leviticus 17:11 states:

> [11] *For the life of a creature is in the blood, and I have given it to you to make atonement for yourselves on the altar; it is the blood that makes atonement for one's life. –Leviticus 17:11 NIV*

Because the blood of the sacrifice had been poured out, covering the people's sin, the nation of Israel could now experience fellowship with Yahweh.

THE BLOOD SACRIFICES
WERE LIKE A CREDIT CARD

The blood sacrifices prescribed in the Hebrew Bible could never really take away sin. (Hebrews chapters 9-10) Instead, these sacrifices were like a credit card. A credit card has no intrinsic value of its own, but the reason the merchant accepts it as payment for goods is because he knows that real payment is coming. So it was with the sacrifices offered in the Tabernacle and the Temple. They were like a credit card, having no real value in and of themselves; they were merely a shadow of the real payment that was coming in the person of Yeshua HaMashiach (Jesus the Messiah).

> [1]*For the Law, since it has only a shadow of the good things to come and not the very form of things, can never, by the same sacrifices which they offer continually year by year, make perfect those who draw near. ~Hebrews 10:1 NASB*

> [17]*things which are a mere shadow of what is to come; but the substance belongs to (Messiah). ~Colossians 2:17 NASB*

The Law was the shadow, and Yeshua is the substance. The sacrifices formally offered in the Tabernacle and then later in the Temple were a shadow, a symbol, and a type of Yeshua. Yeshua's sacrificial death and shed blood on the cross was the final blood sacrifice needed, bringing the Levitical sacrificial system to its ultimate fulfillment.

TORAH PRESCRIBED BLOOD SACRIFICIAL SYSTEM ENDS

In large measure, the Judaism of today is not the religion that the ancient Israelites of the Hebrew scriptures practiced. In the year 70 CE (Common Era), the Romans came into Jerusalem and destroyed the Temple and scattered the Israelites' priesthood. Without the Temple and the priesthood, the Jewish people could no longer offer to Yahweh the blood sacrifices prescribed in the

Torah. (These blood sacrifices are outlined in the book of Leviticus.)

As a result of no longer having a Temple, sacrifices, and a functioning Levitical priesthood, the religion that Yahweh gave the ancient Israelites could no longer be fully practiced. In response to this problem, the religious leaders of that day got together and reinvented Judaism between 70 CE and 130 CE. This reinvention of Judaism is known as Rabbinic or Orthodox Judaism, which is the religion of observant Jews today. As I stated, the blood sacrifices, which are outlined and prescribed in the book of Leviticus, are not practiced by today's Orthodox Jewish community.

I believe that the reason the God of Israel allowed the Temple, Levitical priesthood, and blood sacrifices to come to an end, is because Yeshua's death made them no longer necessary. The fact that the LORD intended for the Levitical system of sacrifice to end at Yeshua's death was revealed, when the veil separating the Holy Place from the Holy of Holies was supernaturally torn in half from top to bottom, when Yeshua breathed His last breath.

> [50]*And Jesus cried out again with a loud voice, and yielded up His spirit.* [51]*And behold, the veil of the temple was torn in two from top to bottom;* ~Matthew 27:50-51a NASB

This cataclysmic supernatural event signified that a new era had come. With the tearing of the veil at Yeshua's death, God was communicating that all mankind could now have access into His presence through Yeshua.

Ever since Yahweh allowed the Temple to be destroyed in 70 CE, the Jewish people haven't been able to offer blood sacrifices. Since they no longer have the Temple, and since they no longer have the priesthood, and since they no longer have the animal sacrifices, the only blood atonement left for

<u>them is Yeshua.</u> He ultimately is the fulfillment of the blood sacrificial system.

YESHUA – MEDIATOR
BETWEEN MANKIND AND GOD

Yeshua brought blood atonement for sin to its completion. Through the shedding of His blood, mankind, once and for all, can find forgiveness of sin by placing their trust in Him. Yeshua became the mediator between mankind and God.

Some Jewish people today claim they have no need for a mediator between themselves and God. They believe they can go directly to God. The truth of the matter is, in biblical Judaism, the Jewish nation never went directly to God. The priesthood always served as a mediator between the Jewish people and God.

When a sacrifice was brought to Yahweh, an Israelite couldn't offer the sacrifice directly to God; instead, the sacrifice was brought to the priest, and the priest offered the sacrifice to Yahweh on the worshipper's behalf.

We see this truth clearly revealed on Yom Kippur (the Day of Atonement) when <u>only</u> the High Priest could enter the Holy of Holies in the Tabernacle/Temple to offer atonement for Israel's sin. (Leviticus 16) There has always been a mediator in Judaism between mankind and God; Yeshua has now become that mediator.

> [10]*we have been made holy through the sacrifice of the body of Jesus (Messiah) once for all. ~Hebrews 10:10b NIV*

> [5]*For there is one God, and one mediator also between God and men, the man (Messiah) Jesus, ~1 Timothy 2:5 NASB*

JEWISH PEOPLE TODAY ARE
MORE OPEN TO ACCEPT YESHUA

As society has been changing, so have the walls of separation between Jew and Gentile. We now see Jewish people marrying outside of their faith at approximately 50%. Many more Jewish people are becoming receptive to receive the Good News of Yeshua than they were just 50 years ago. Even in Israel, Jewish people are coming to accept Yeshua at such a rapid pace that there aren't enough people to keep up with discipling them.

> [37]*"The harvest is plentiful but the workers are few.* [38]*Ask the LORD of the harvest, therefore, to send out workers into his harvest field." ~Matthew 9:37b-38 NIV*

This plentiful harvest of Jewish believers is leading up to and preparing the way for Yeshua's magnificent and glorious return. If you are a Gentile believer, you have been chosen by God and have been given the wonderful privilege of proclaiming to the Jewish people that Yeshua is their Messiah. You must tell your Jewish friend that Judaism without Yeshua is insufficient.

TO MY BELOVED JEWISH FRIENDS

The following is a true account of a Jewish man who received Yeshua as his Messiah. This Jewish man was in the United States armed forces and was stationed in Alaska as a barracks captain. One of the men assigned to his barracks was a short Italian man who was a believer in Yeshua. The other soldiers in the barracks constantly harassed this Italian man, because he was a believer. All the soldiers would go out drinking and partying, except for this Italian believer. He tried to live a clean life and was truly focused on his walk with God. While the others were gone, he would stay in the barracks and read his Bible.

One day some of the soldiers in the barracks pinned the believer on the ground and forcibly opened his mouth, pouring scotch down his throat, to get him drunk. The Jewish man, who was in charge of keeping order in the barracks, felt the only way to protect this Italian believer was to keep him separate from the large common barracks room. So the Jewish barracks captain brought him into his private quarters.

As time went on, the Italian believer respectfully began to question the Jewish man. He asked him, "What do you think about Isaiah 53? Does this scripture relate to Jesus?" The believer's questions troubled the Jewish man, so he made an appointment to see his rabbi. The Jewish man asked his rabbi, "What is Isaiah 53 about?" Immediately, the rabbi said, "It's not about Jesus." When the rabbi made that statement, the Jewish man thought, "Oh, God, he's afraid it might be Jesus, too."

After speaking to the rabbi, he thought to himself, "I'm just going to forget all this Jesus stuff. I'm not going to let it bother me anymore. I'm going to put it completely out of my mind." That night, however, Jesus appeared to him in a dream, saying, "Three signs will happen, and when they happen, you will know I'm the Messiah."

The first of the three signs was that someone would try to attack him, but God would save him. A few days later, when he was taking a shower, someone came into the shower stall to attack him, but when he called upon God, others came in and prevented it from happening.

The second of the three signs was that someone he greatly esteemed with a very high rank would be demoted. A short time later, when he was in the laundry room, a previously high-ranking officer came in, and the uniform he was now wearing showed he had been significantly demoted.

The last of the three signs that was given to him was that he would see Jesus. A couple of weeks later, right before his time of duty ended, he went to a Christian movie, only because he had nothing else to do, and it was free. While he was watching the movie, suddenly the face of the actor, who was portraying Jesus, turned into the face of Jesus, who had appeared to him in the dream, giving him the three signs. When this occurred, He didn't know what was happening. He kept closing and reopening his eyes trying to clear his vision, but all he saw was the face of the Jesus, who had appeared to him in his dream, who had said to him, "Three signs will happen, and when they happen, you will know I am the Messiah."

After those three signs came to pass, that Jewish man became a believer in Jesus, and today he is a Messianic rabbi. Just as Jesus revealed Himself to this Jewish man, He desires to reveal Himself to you, so you will recognize Him as your Messiah.

Chapter Four

Messianic Prophecy

WHO IS HAMASHIACH (THE MESSIAH)?

I am a Jew who believes Yeshua is the Messiah the Hebrew prophets spoke of in the Hebrew Bible (Old Testament). When I share the message of Yeshua with other Jews, I am not calling them out of Judaism or trying to convert them to some other religion. I'm proclaiming Yeshua to be the Messiah, who is revealed in the Hebrew Bible, and that He is the fulfillment of Judaism. Yeshua is the fulfillment of the Law and the Prophets. He emphasized that He didn't come to abolish them but to fulfill them and bring them to their fullest meaning.

> [17]*"Do not think that I have come to abolish the Law or the Prophets; I have not come to abolish them but to fulfill them." ~Matthew 5:17 NIV*

MESSIANIC PROPHECIES

In the Hebrew Bible (Old Testament), the Hebrew prophets gave detailed information about the Messiah: where He would be born, what He would look like, and the events that would take place when He came. We will look at many of these prophecies and then show how they are fulfilled in Yeshua.

Yeshua made it very clear that the entire Hebrew Bible pointed to and prophesied of Him. This is illustrated in Luke 24:13-27. As you read this account of scripture below, pay particular attention to verse 27 which makes this point clear.

[13]And behold, two of them were going that very day to a village named Emmaus, which was about seven miles from Jerusalem. [14]And they were talking with each other about all these things which had taken place. [15]While they were talking and discussing, Jesus Himself approached and began traveling with them. [16]But their eyes were prevented from recognizing Him. [17]And He said to them, "What are these words that you are exchanging with one another as you are walking?" And they stood still, looking sad. [18]One of them, named Cleopas, answered and said to Him, "Are You the only one visiting Jerusalem and unaware of the things which have happened here in these days?" [19]And He said to them, "What things?" And they said to Him, "The things about Jesus the Nazarene, who was a prophet mighty in deed and word in the sight of God and all the people, [20]and how the chief priests and our rulers delivered Him to the sentence of death, and crucified Him. [21]But we were hoping that it was He who was going to redeem

Israel. Indeed, besides all this, it is the third day since these things happened. ²²But also some women among us amazed us. When they were at the tomb early in the morning, ²³and did not find His body, they came, saying that they had also seen a vision of angels who said that He was alive. ²⁴Some of those who were with us went to the tomb and found it just exactly as the women also had said; but Him they did not see." ²⁵And He said to them, "O foolish men and slow of heart to believe in all that the prophets have spoken! ²⁶Was it not necessary for the (Messiah) to suffer these things and to enter into His glory?" ²⁷Then beginning with Moses and with all the prophets, He explained to them the things concerning Himself in all the Scriptures. ⌐Luke 24:13-27 NASB

DEUTERONOMY 18:15

The Hebrew prophet Moses (Moshe) declared that God would bring forth a prophet from the Jewish nation, who would be like himself.

¹⁵The LORD your God will raise up for you a prophet like me from among your own brothers. You must listen to him. ⌐Deuteronomy 18:15 NIV

Yeshua proclaims He is the prophet of whom Moses prophesied.

⁴⁶"If you believed Moses, you would believe me, for he wrote about me." ⌐John 5:46 NIV

ISAIAH 52:14-15a

The Hebrew prophet Isaiah (Yesh`ayahu) prophesied the Messiah would come as a servant and accomplish many great things; in doing so, His appearance would become disfigured.

> [14]*Just as there were many who were appalled at him—his appearance was so disfigured beyond that of any man and his form marred beyond human likeness—* [15]*so will he sprinkle many nations, and kings will shut their mouths because of him.* -Isaiah 52:14-15a NIV

It is unfortunate that so few Jewish people have seen the movie, *The Passion*. It vividly portrays what happened to Yeshua when He was beaten, whipped, spit on, and eventually put to death on the cross. Rabbis warned the Jewish people not to see the movie, but my Jewish brothers and sisters shouldn't be afraid to expose themselves to the truth.

From the time Adam and Eve sinned in the Garden of Eden, there has been a separation of mankind from a holy God. In order to have a relationship with God, sin had to be dealt with; therefore, God designed a sacrificial system to deal with man's sin. This sacrificial system is described in the book of Leviticus in the Torah. Worshippers were required to bring an unblemished animal to the priest to be sacrificed. The worshipper would place his hands on the head of the animal, thus transferring his sin into it. The animal would then be put to death and its blood smeared on the altar. Only then could the worshipper have fellowship with God.

Yeshua, the unblemished Lamb of God, died and shed His blood as the sacrifice for the forgiveness of sin for all mankind. Now, through Yeshua, we are able to have fellowship with God. He is the fulfillment of the sacrificial system, and in fulfilling it, His appearance was disfigured.

ISAIAH 53

The most famous prophecy of Messiah in the Hebrew Bible is Isaiah 53. This incredible prophecy foretold the coming of Messiah as a suffering servant, bearing upon Himself the sins of the world and sacrificially dying for all mankind. It speaks of the Jewish people's failure to recognize their Messiah and their ultimate rejection of Him.

Isaiah 53 isn't even read in most synagogues. It's a shame and a tragedy that this section of scripture isn't taught. I believe one of the reasons that this section of scripture isn't taught, frankly, is because rabbis don't want to expose their congregants to it, because they're afraid they might end up wondering if Yeshua is the Messiah. Well, I have news for you, Yeshua is the Messiah! My Jewish brothers and sisters, look to Adonai, the God of Israel, and ask Him, "God of Avraham (Abraham), Yitzak (Isaac), and Yaakov (Jacob), is Yeshua the Messiah?" If Isaiah 53 is read with an open mind, a Jewish person will see that it can only refer to Yeshua, even though the rabbis would like them to believe that it refers to something else.

ISAIAH 53:1

Isaiah prophesied that most Jewish people would not believe Messiah's message, as is the case today. Most Jewish people, from the time of Yeshua, even until today, have not been able to see that Yeshua is the Messiah. The scriptures teach that there is a veil over their eyes.

> [1]*Who has believed our message and to whom has the arm of the LORD been revealed? ~Isaiah 53:1 NIV*

But although the majority of Jewish people in Yeshua's day did not recognize Him as the Messiah, thousands did. In the B'rit Chadashah (New Testament), we read that there were thousands of Jews who believed Yeshua was the Messiah, even some Jewish priests and rulers.

> [20]*When they heard this, they praised God. Then they said to Paul: "You see, brother, how many thousands of Jews have believed, and all of them are zealous for the law." ~Acts 21:20 NIV*

> [7]*So the word of God spread. The number of disciples in Jerusalem increased rapidly, and a large number of priests became obedient to the faith. ~Acts 6:7 NIV*

ISAIAH 53:2-3

Isaiah prophesied there would be nothing about Messiah's appearance which would attract us to Him, and He would suffer, being despised and rejected by men.

> [2]*He grew up before him like a tender shoot, and like a root out of dry ground. He had no beauty or majesty to attract us to him, nothing in his appearance that we should desire him.* [3]*He was despised and rejected by men, a man of sorrows, and familiar with suffering. Like one from whom men hide their faces, he was despised, and we esteemed him not. ~Isaiah 53:2-3 NIV*

Yeshua fulfilled this prophecy when He was rejected by His own people.

> [11]*He came to that which was his own, but his own did not receive him. ~John 1:11 NIV*

Yeshua was also rejected by the religious leaders of His day, the Pharisees and Sadducees. They hated and despised Him, because He threatened their position and power.

> [48]*"What are we accomplishing?" they asked. "Here is this man performing many miraculous signs. If we let him go on like this, everyone will believe in him, and then the Romans will come and take away both our place and our nation." ~John 11:48 NIV*

ISAIAH 53:4

Isaiah prophesied that we would believe that Messiah was being afflicted by God, even though in reality, He was being afflicted for us.

> [4]*Surely he took up our infirmities and carried our sorrows, yet we considered him stricken by God, smitten by him, and afflicted. ~Isaiah 53:4 NIV*

Yeshua fulfilled this prophecy, even as the people ridiculed Him, while He was dying on the cross for their sins.

> [39]*Those who passed by hurled insults at him, shaking their heads* [40]*and saying, "You who are going to destroy the temple and build it in three days, save yourself! Come down from the cross, if you are the Son of God!"* [41]*In the same way the chief priests, the teachers of the*

law and the elders mocked him. ⁴²*"He saved others,"*
they said, "but he can't save himself! He's the King of
Israel! Let him come down now from the cross, and we
will believe in him." ~Matthew 27:39-42 NIV

ISAIAH 53:5-6

Isaiah prophesied that Messiah would be pierced for our
transgressions.

⁵*But he was pierced for our transgressions, he was*
crushed for our iniquities; the punishment that brought
us peace was upon him, and by his wounds we are
healed. ⁶*We all, like sheep, have gone astray, each of us*
has turned to his own way, and the LORD has laid on
him the iniquity of us all. ~Isaiah 53:5-6 NIV

Yeshua fulfilled this prophecy when a soldier took a
spear and pierced His side after He died on the cross.
The blood which flowed out from His side was for our
transgressions.

³⁴*Instead, one of the soldiers pierced Jesus' side with*
a spear, bringing a sudden flow of blood and water.
~John 19:34 NIV

Yeshua and the New Testament writers taught that
His death and shed blood were the fulfillment of Isaiah's
prophecy.

²⁴*He himself bore our sins in his body on the tree, ... by*
his wounds you have been healed. ~1 Peter 2:24 NIV

ISAIAH 53:7

Isaiah prophesied that Messiah would be oppressed and afflicted, yet He would not open His mouth.

> [7] *He was oppressed and afflicted, yet he did not open his mouth; he was led like a lamb to the slaughter, and as a sheep before her shearers is silent, so he did not open his mouth. ~Isaiah 53:7 NIV*

Yeshua fulfilled this prophecy when He remained silent as Pontius Pilate questioned Him before His crucifixion.

> [11] *Meanwhile Jesus stood before the governor, and the governor asked him, "Are you the king of the Jews?" "Yes, it is as you say," Jesus replied.* [12] *When he was accused by the chief priests and the elders, he gave no answer.* [13] *Then Pilate asked him, "Don't you hear the testimony they are bringing against you?"* [14] *But Jesus made no reply, not even to a single charge—to the great amazement of the governor. ~Matthew 27:11-14 NIV*

ISAIAH 53:7b-8a

Isaiah prophesied that Messiah would be led as a lamb to the slaughter.

> [7] *he was led like a lamb to the slaughter, and as a sheep before her shearers is silent, so he did not open His mouth.* [8] *By oppression and judgment he was taken away. ~Isaiah 53:7b-8a NIV*

Yeshua fulfilled this prophecy when He was taken away to be crucified.

¹⁶*Finally Pilate handed him over to them to be crucified. ~John 19:16 NIV*

ISAIAH 53:8b

Isaiah prophesied that Messiah would die for the transgression of the people.

⁸*And who can speak of his descendants? For he was cut off from the land of the living; for the transgression of my people he was stricken. ~Isaiah 53:8b NIV*

Yeshua fulfilled this prophecy when He was crucified. The Jewish religious leaders and Roman authorities thought they were just getting rid of a troublemaker, but it was all God's plan for Yeshua to take our sin in His own body and die for us. He gave His life for ours, absorbing our sin in His body, as portrayed in the sacrificial system revealed in the Torah in the book of Leviticus. Yeshua shed His blood, so we could have forgiveness of sin and a relationship with Yahweh, the God of Israel.

ISAIAH 53:9

Isaiah prophesied that Messiah would be buried in a rich man's tomb.

⁹*He was assigned a grave with the wicked, and with the rich in his death, though he had done no violence, nor was any deceit in his mouth. ~Isaiah 53:9 NIV*

Yeshua fulfilled this prophecy when He was buried in the tomb of Joseph, a rich man from Arimathea.

⁵⁷As evening approached, there came a rich man from Arimathea, named Joseph, who had himself become a disciple of Jesus. ⁵⁸Going to Pilate, he asked for Jesus' body, and Pilate ordered that it be given to him. ⁵⁹Joseph took the body, wrapped it in a clean linen cloth, ⁶⁰and placed it in his own new tomb that he had cut out of the rock. He rolled a big stone in front of the entrance to the tomb and went away. ~Matthew 27:57-60 NIV

ISAIAH 53:12

Isaiah prophesied that Messiah would be numbered with the transgressors.

¹²and was numbered with the transgressors... ~Isaiah 53:12b NIV

Yeshua fulfilled this prophecy when He was crucified between two criminals.

³⁸Two robbers were crucified with him, one on his right and one on his left. ~Matthew 27:38 NIV

PSALM 22

Psalm 22 is a Messianic prophecy which undoubtedly points to Yeshua. As you read it, do so through the eyes of Yeshua on the cross.

Messianic Rabbi K. A. Schneider

PSALM 22:1

The prophecy contained in the first verse declares that Messiah will be forsaken by God.

> ¹*My God, my God, why have you forsaken me? Why are you so far from saving me, so far from the words of my groaning? ~Psalm 22:1 NIV*

Yeshua fulfilled this prophecy when He spoke these words while He hung dying on the cross:

> ⁴⁶*About the ninth hour Jesus cried out in a loud voice, "Eloi, Eloi, lama sabachthani?"—which means, "My God, my God, why have you forsaken me?" ~Matthew 27:46 NIV*

PSALM 22:2-8

The following verses prophesy that Messiah will be mocked and insulted.

> ²*O my God, I cry out by day, but you do not answer, by night, and am not silent. ³Yet you are enthroned as the Holy One; you are the praise of Israel. ⁴In you our fathers put their trust; they trusted and you delivered them. ⁵They cried to you and were saved; in you they trusted and were not disappointed. ⁶But I am a worm and not a man, scorned by men and despised by the people. ⁷All who see me mock me; they hurl insults, shaking their heads: ⁸"He trusts in the LORD; let the LORD rescue him. Let him deliver him, since he delights in him." ~Psalm 22:2-8 NIV*

Yeshua's fulfillment of this prophecy is recorded in Matthew 27:39-44, when He was mocked and insulted as He hung on the cross.

> [39]*Those who passed by hurled insults at him, shaking their heads* [40]*and saying, "You who are going to destroy the temple and build it in three days, save yourself! Come down from the cross, if you are the Son of God!"* [41]*In the same way the chief priests, the teachers of the law and the elders mocked him.* [42]*"He saved others,"* *they said, "but he can't save himself! He's the King of Israel! Let him come down now from the cross, and we will believe in him.* [43]*He trusts in God. Let God rescue him now if he wants him, for he said, 'I am the Son of God.'"* [44]*In the same way the robbers who were crucified with him also heaped insults on him.* ~Matthew 27:39-44 NIV

PSALM 22:9-15

This prophecy speaks of Messiah thirsting as He is dying.

[9]*Yet you brought me out of the womb; you made me trust in you even at my mother's breast.* [10]*From birth I was cast upon you; from my mother's womb you have been my God.* [11]*Do not be far from me, for trouble is near and there is no one to help.* [12]*Many bulls surround me; strong bulls of Bashan encircle me.* [13]*Roaring lions tearing their prey open their mouths wide against me.* [14]*I am poured out like water, and all my bones are out of joint. My heart has turned to wax; it has melted away within me.* [15]*My strength is dried up like a potsherd,*

*and my tongue sticks to the roof of my mouth; you lay
me in the dust of death. ~Psalm 22:9-15 NIV*

Yeshua fulfilled this prophecy as He thirsted while
dying on the cross.

*[28]Later, knowing that all was now completed, and
so that the Scripture would be fulfilled, Jesus said, "I
am thirsty." [29]A jar of wine vinegar was there, so they
soaked a sponge in it, put the sponge on a stalk of the
hyssop plant, and lifted it to Jesus' lips. ~John 19:28-
29 NIV*

PSALM 22:16

Verse 16 prophesies that Messiah will be surrounded by
evil men and have His hands and feet pierced.

*[16]Dogs have surrounded me; a band of evil men has
encircled me, they have pierced my hands and my feet.
~Psalm 22:16 NIV*

Yeshua fulfilled this prophecy when the Roman soldiers
nailed His hands and feet to the cross. After He rose from
the dead, Thomas declared that he needed to see the nail
marks in Yeshua's skin in order to believe.

*[25]So the other disciples told him, "We have seen the
Lord!" But he said to them, "Unless I see the nail
marks in his hands and put my finger where the nails
were, and put my hand into his side, I will not believe
it." ~John 20:25 NIV*

PSALM 22:17

The prophecy in verse 17 describes how the people will stare and gloat over Messiah.

> ¹⁷*I can count all my bones; people stare and gloat over me. ~Psalm 22:17 NIV*

Yeshua fulfilled this prophecy while large numbers of people watched His crucifixion, some of them gloating over Him.

> ²⁷*A large number of people followed him, including women who mourned and wailed for him. ~Luke 23:27 NIV*

> ³⁵*The people stood watching, and the rulers even sneered at him. They said, "He saved others; let him save himself if he is the (Messiah) of God, the Chosen One." ~Luke 23:35 NIV*

PSALM 22:18

Verse 18 prophesies that Messiah's garments will be divided amongst those casting lots.

> ¹⁸*They divide my garments among them and cast lots for my clothing. ~Psalm 22:18 NIV*

Yeshua fulfilled this prophecy when the Roman soldiers crucifying Him casted lots for His clothes.

> ³⁵*When they had crucified him, they divided up his clothes by casting lots. ~Matthew 27:35 NIV*

PSALM 22:19-31

The remainder of the 22nd chapter of Psalms describes how Messiah will be praised and worshipped by many because of what He has done.

19But you, O LORD, be not far off; O my Strength, come quickly to help me. 20Deliver my life from the sword, my precious life from the power of the dogs. 21Rescue me from the mouth of the lions; save me from the horns of the wild oxen. 22I will declare your name to my brothers; in the congregation I will praise you. 23You who fear the LORD, praise him! All you descendants of Jacob, honor him! Revere him, all you descendants of Israel! 24For he has not despised or disdained the suffering of the afflicted one; he has not hidden his face from him but has listened to his cry for help. 25From you comes the theme of my praise in the great assembly; before those who fear you will I fulfill my vows. 26The poor will eat and be satisfied; they who seek the LORD will praise him—may your hearts live forever! 27All the ends of the earth will remember and turn to the LORD, and all the families of the nations will bow down before him, 28for dominion belongs to the LORD and he rules over the nations. 29All the rich of the earth will feast and worship; all who go down to the dust will kneel before him—those who cannot keep themselves alive. 30Posterity will serve him; future generations will be told about the LORD. 31They will proclaim his righteousness to a people yet unborn—for he has done it. ~Psalm 22:19-31 NIV

Yeshua fulfilled this prophecy by triumphantly overcoming the power of sin and death by His own death and resurrection; subsequently, all nations will bow before

Him. All generations of the earth will exalt God in praise and worship for the deliverance they receive through Yeshua, even as millions and millions and millions through the ages already have.

> ⁹*Therefore God exalted him to the highest place and gave him the name that is above every name, ¹⁰that at the name of Jesus every knee should bow, in heaven and on earth and under the earth, ¹¹and every tongue confess that Jesus (Messiah) is Lord, to the glory of God the Father. ~Philippians 2:9-11 NIV*

ISAIAH 7:14

The prophet Isaiah foretold of a virgin giving birth to a child who would be called Immanuel (God with us). This child would literally be God born in human flesh.

> ¹⁴*Therefore the LORD himself will give you a sign: The virgin will be with child and will give birth to a son, and will call him Immanuel. ~Isaiah 7:14 NIV*

Yeshua fulfilled this prophecy when He was born of a virgin and was called Immanuel.

> ²¹*"She will give birth to a son, and you are to give him the name Jesus, because he will save his people from their sins." ²²All this took place to fulfill what the LORD had said through the prophet: ²³"The virgin will be with child and will give birth to a son, and they will call him Immanuel"—which means, "God with us." ~Matthew 1:21-23 NIV*

MICAH 5:2

The Hebrew prophet Micah (Mikhah) prophesied that Messiah would be born in Bethlehem, and He would come from ancient of times. In other words, He wouldn't be an ordinary human being; He would be God.

> [2]*"But you, Bethlehem Ephrathah, though you are small among the clans of Judah, out of you will come for me one who will be ruler over Israel, whose origins are from of old, from ancient times." ~Micah 5:2 NIV*

Yeshua fulfilled this prophecy by being born in Bethlehem.

> [1]*After Jesus was born in Bethlehem in Judea, during the time of King Herod, Magi from the east came to Jerusalem ~Matthew 2:1 NIV*

ISAIAH 11:1-2

Isaiah prophesied that Messiah would come from the lineage of Jesse.

> [1]*A shoot will come up from the stump of Jesse; from his roots a Branch will bear fruit.* [2]*The Spirit of the LORD will rest on him — the Spirit of wisdom and of understanding, the Spirit of counsel and of power, the Spirit of knowledge and of the fear of the LORD - ~Isaiah 11:1-2 NIV*

Yeshua fulfilled this prophecy by being born through David, the son of Jesse. The B'rit Chadashah (New Testament) begins by tracing Yeshua's genealogy back to David, the son of Abraham, with the very first verse.

¹*A record of the genealogy of Jesus (Messiah) the son of David, the son of Abraham: ~Matthew 1:1 NIV*

ISAIAH 11:10-11

Isaiah prophesied that many nations would rally to the Messiah.

¹⁰*In that day the Root of Jesse will stand as a banner for the peoples; the nations will rally to him, and his place of rest will be glorious. ¹¹In that day the LORD will reach out his hand a second time to reclaim the remnant that is left of his people from Assyria, from Lower Egypt, from Upper Egypt, from Cush, from Elam, from Babylonia, from Hamath and from the islands of the sea. ~Isaiah 11:10-11 NIV*

Yeshua has fulfilled this prophecy as many nations of the world have rallied to Him and continue rallying to Him. All the nations of the world, Jew and Gentile alike, are coming together to become one in Messiah.

⁶*This mystery is that through the gospel the Gentiles are heirs together with Israel, members together of one body, and sharers together in the promise in (Messiah) Jesus. ~Ephesians 3:6 NIV*

ZECHARIAH 12:10

The Hebrew prophet, Zechariah (Zekharyah), prophesied that the Jewish people would one day look upon Messiah, the One they pierced, and they would mourn and grieve for Him.

> ¹⁰*And I will pour out on the house of David and the inhabitants of Jerusalem a spirit of grace and supplication. They will look on me, the one they have pierced, and they will mourn for him as one mourns for an only child, and grieve bitterly for him as one grieves for a firstborn son. ~Zechariah 12:10 NIV*

Yeshua will one day fulfill Zechariah's prophecy as recorded in the book of Revelation.

> ⁷*Look, he is coming with the clouds, and every eye will see him, even those who pierced him; and all the peoples of the earth will mourn because of him. So shall it be! Amen. ~Revelation 1:7 NIV*

ISRAEL'S FAILURE TO RECOGNIZE THE MESSIAH

The God of Israel revealed many details concerning the Messiah to the nation of Israel through the Hebrew prophets. Even though Yeshua fulfilled all of these numerous prophecies, many have failed to recognize Him as the prophesied Messiah. Yeshua is indeed the Messiah and the fulfillment of Judaism, but only God Himself can make this known to an individual. Yeshua said in John 6:44, "No one can come to Me unless the Father who sent Me draws him."

Below you will find a partial list of the many prophecies from the Hebrew Bible that Yeshua fulfilled.

Messianic Prophecies and Their Fulfillments

Description	Hebrew Bible Prophecy	NT Fulfillment
Messiah will be the offspring of a woman	Genesis 3:15	Luke 2:4-11 Galatians 4:4
Messiah will be the seed of Abraham	Genesis 22:18	Matthew 1:1
Messiah will be a descendant of Isaac	Genesis 21:12	Matthew 1:1-2
Messiah will be the offspring of Abraham, Isaac, and Jacob	Genesis 17:19 Numbers 24:17	Luke 3:34 Matthew 1:2
Messiah will be of the tribe of Judah	Genesis 49:10	Matthew 1:1-2
Messiah will be a descendant of David	Jeremiah 23:5	Matthew 1:1, 6 Revelation 22:16
Messiah is the Son of God	Psalm 2:7	Matthew 17:5 Luke 3:38 Luke 22:70
Messiah will be taken to Egypt	Hosea 11:1	Matthew 2:14-15

Messiah will be preceded by a messenger	Malachi 3:1	John 1:23 Matthew 3:1-3 Matthew 11:14
Messiah's ministry will be in Galilee	Isaiah 9:1	Matthew 4:12-17
Messiah will perform miracles	Isaiah 35:5-6	Matthew 9:35
Messiah will preach good news	Isaiah 61:1	Luke 4:14-21
Messiah will teach parables	Psalm 78:2	Matthew 13:34-35
Messiah will minister to Gentiles	Isaiah 42:1 Isaiah 49:1	Luke 2:32
Messiah will be a light to the Gentiles	Isaiah 60:3	Acts 13:47-48
Messiah will be hated without cause	Psalm 69:4	John 15:24-25
Messiah will be rejected by His own people	Psalm 31:11 Psalm 118:22	John 1:11 1 Peter 2:7
Messiah will enter Jerusalem triumphantly on a donkey	Zechariah 9:9	Matthew 21:1-9 Luke 19:28-37 John 12:12-16

Messiah will be betrayed by one of His followers	Psalm 41:9	Matthew 26:47-50 Luke 22:47-48 John 18:1-6
Messiah will be betrayed for 30 pieces of silver	Zechariah 11:12	Matthew 26:14-15
Messiah will be struck and spat on by His enemies	Isaiah 50:6	Matthew 26:67 Matthew 27:30 Mark 14:65
Messiah will be given vinegar and gall	Psalm 69:21	Matthew 27:34 John 19:28-30
Messiah's bones will not be broken	Exodus 12:46 Psalm 34:20	John 19:31-36
Messiah will rise from the dead	Psalm 16:10 Hosea 6:2	Acts 2:22-32 Matthew 28:1-10
Messiah is now at God's right hand	Psalm 110:1	Mark 16:19 Luke 24:50-51
Messiah will be a priest	Psalm 110:4	Hebrews 5:5, 6 Hebrews 3:1
Messiah is eternal	Isaiah 9:6	John 8:58 John 1:1
Messiah will be King	Zechariah 9:9	John 18:33-38 Matthew 27:37

www.DiscoveringTheJewishJesus.com